THE 2023 WINNING

BIPOLAR PROTOCOL

The fool proof nutritional guide to support mood stability and improve your mental well-being

Dr Lizzy Evans

The 2023 WINNING BIPOLAR DIET PROTOCOL

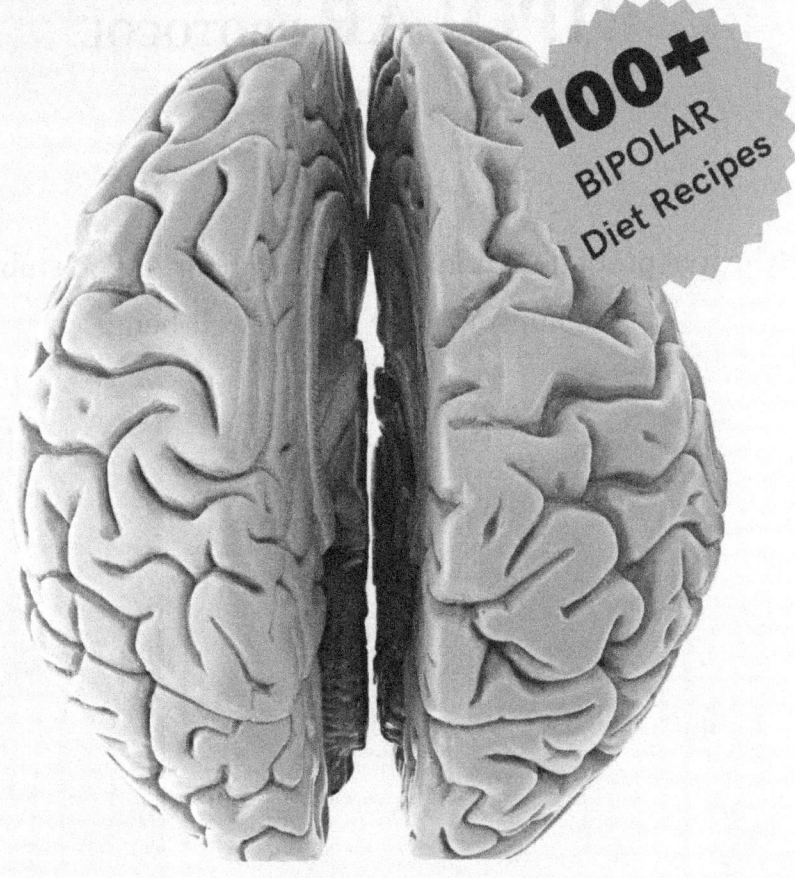

100+ BIPOLAR Diet Recipes

DR Lizzy Evans

Copyright Page

Copyright © 2023 by Lizzy Evans M.D. All rights reserved. Manufactured in the United States of America. The reproduction or distribution of any part of this publication, in any form or by any means, or its storage in a database or retrieval system, without the prior written permission of the publisher, is strictly prohibited under the United States Copyright Act of 1976.

All trademarks mentioned in this book are the property of their respective owners. The use of these trademarks is purely editorial and does not imply any endorsement or infringement of the trademark rights. Trademarked names appearing in this book are printed with initial caps.

TERMS OF USE: This work, authored by Lizzy Evans and its licensors, is protected by copyright laws. All rights are reserved. Your use of this work is subject to the following terms: Except as permitted under the Copyright Act of 1976, you are prohibited from decompiling, disassembling, reverse engineering, reproducing, modifying, creating derivative works based upon, transmitting, distributing, disseminating, selling, publishing, or sublicensing the work or any part of it without prior consent from McGraw-Hill.

You are permitted to store and retrieve one copy of the work for your own noncommercial and personal use. Any other use of the work is strictly prohibited. Failure to comply with these terms may result in the termination of your right to use the work.

The thoughts, methods, and suggestions presented in this book reflect the authors' opinions and experiences. They have been developed to the best of their knowledge and with utmost care. However, they should not be considered a substitute for personal and competent medical advice. Each reader is responsible for their actions and decisions. Neither the author nor the publisher can be held liable for any disadvantages or damages arising from the practical information provided in this book.

Table of Contents

Copyright Page 3

Table of Contents 5

Understanding Bipolar Disorder 1

    Prevalence and impact of bipolar disorder 3

    Types of bipolar disorder 4

    Symptoms and Diagnosis of Bipolar Disorder 6

    Diagnostic criteria for bipolar disorder 7

    Causes and Risk Factors 9

    Genetic factors 11

    Environmental factors 12

    Brain chemistry and structure 14

    Risk Factors for Bipolar Disorder 15

The Bipolar Treatment Options 17

    Medication 18

    Psychotherapy 20

    Lifestyle changes 21

Living with Bipolar Disorder 23

Coping strategies 24

Managing relationships 26

Career considerations for people with bipolar disorder 28

Stigma and Misconceptions for people with bipolar disorder 29

Common myths about bipolar disorder 31

Reducing stigma and improving understanding 33

Future Research and Directions 34

Bipolar Disorder and its Impact on Diet 36

Nutrients for Bipolar Health 37

Nutrients that support bipolar health, such as omega-3 fatty acids, B vitamins, and magnesium 39

Foods to Eat on a Bipolar Diet 40

Foods support brain health and mood regulation 42

Foods to Avoid on a Bipolar Diet 43

Foods can contribute to mood instability and inflammation 45

30 Days Sample Meal Plan for a Bipolar Diet 47

BREAKFAST RECIPES FOR BIPOLAR DISORDER 47

Bread Bowl Quiche 47

Vegetarian Breakfast Apple Sausages 49

Sweet Potato Breakfast Cups 52

Thanksgiving Leftover Sweet Potato Waffles 56

Pineapple Carrot Cake Breakfast Bread 59

Easy Cast-Iron Cheesy Asparagus Quiche 62

High-Protein Sweet And Savory Crepes 64

Garden Vegetable Vegan Quiche 68

Eggs In Purgatory 72

Steak And Eggs Hash 74

Stocked Brooklyn's Sweet Potato "Toast" 77

Almond Butter Cucumber Crunch Sandwich 80

Southwestern One-pan Shakshuka 81

Egg, Avocado, & Tomato Toast 83

Pear & Honey Sweet Potato Toast 84

Chickpea Flour Omelet 85

Protein-Packed Breakfast Bars 88

Simple Shakshuka 92

Breakfast Taco Cups 94

Broccoli Cheddar Brunch Bake 95

LUNCH RECIPES FOR BIPOLAR DISORDER 98

Mixed Green Salad with Grilled Chicken 98

Veggie Wrap 99

Quinoa and Roasted Vegetable Bowl: 101

Fruit and Spinach Salad: 102

Grilled Vegetable Panini: 103

Chickpea and Vegetable Stir-Fry: 104

Caprese Salad Sandwich: 106

Rainbow Veggie Sushi Rolls: 107

Fruit and Yogurt Parfait 108

Roasted Vegetable and Quinoa Salad: 109

Veggie and Hummus Wrap: 111

Fresh Fruit Salad with Yogurt 112

Sweet Potato and Black Bean Burrito Bowl: 113

Zucchini Noodles with Pesto and Cherry Tomatoes: 114

Spinach and Berry Smoothie Bowl: 116

Mediterranean Chickpea Salad 117

Veggie Quesadillas 118

Rainbow Fruit Skewers with Yogurt Dip: 119

Quinoa and Roasted Vegetable Stuffed Bell Peppers: 120

Greek Salad with Grilled Chicken 122

Veggie and Quinoa Stuffed Portobello Mushrooms 124

DINNER RECIPES FOR BIPOLAR DISORDER 125

Naco Taco 125

Banana Cue 129

Street Corn Empanadas 130

Herby Street Dog Sandwich 133

Watermelon Pistachio Salad 137

Shrimp Summer Salad with Creamy Cilantro Dressing 139

Pineapple Pancetta Pasta 142

Dorm-Friendly Microwave Meals For A Day 144

Salmon Quinoa Bowl 150

Copycat Costco Bulgogi Bake 153

Chai-Spiced Apple Cake 156

Vegan Breakfast Lasagna 159

Filipino Sweet Spaghetti 162

Cranberry And Sage-Stuffed Pork Tenderloin 164

Achiote Turkey 167

Achiote Wings 170

Savory French Toast 174

Carnitas Tostadas With Pineapple Salsa 176

Vanessa's Nicaraguan Carne Asada With Queso Frito 179

Carnitas Tostadas With Pineapple Salsa 182

DESSERTS RECIPES FOR BIPOLAR DISORDER 187

Cardamom-Spiced Carrot Cupcakes 187

Healthy ABC Pudding 191

Citrusy Squash Smash Cake 193

Hamster Cupcakes 195

Butter Beer 197

Stove-Top Cinnamon Apples 199

Pistachio-Orange Thumbprint Cookies with Chocolate Ganache 200

Alix And Zoya's Pride Party 203

Chai-Spiced Apple Cake 208

Ice Spice-Inspired Orange Caramel 211

Unicorn Cookies 213

Ice Cream Bombe 216

Avocado Strawberry Ice Cream 221

Peach Cobbler 222

Vegan Spotted Dick & Custard 226

Snow White Poison Candy Apples 229

6-Hour Salted Caramel Deep Dish Apple Pie 231

Sweet Corn And Blueberry Swirl Ice Cream 236

Magic Fizzy Truffles 238

2-Hour Strawberry Cheesecake 240

SNACK RECIPES FOR BIPOLAR DISORDER 243

Pretzel Bites With Mustard Cheese Sauce 243

Bacon Jam Hacks 245

Mini Strudels 4 Ways 247

Fresh Seacuterie Board 250

Sweet & Spicy Peach Sticky Wings 256

Green Goddess CBD Dip 259

Cucumber Celery Juice 262

Banana Pepper Poppers 264

Back-To-School Snack Board 265

Lumpia (Lumpiang Shanghai) 269

Tasty's Purple Goddess 272

Jasmine's Snack Board 275

Pesto Chicken Low-carb Broccoli Parmesan Cups 280

Protein-Packed Breakfast Bars 282

Easy To Serve Chicken Parmesan Poppers 286

Pizza Nachos 289

Chicken Salad Crostini 292

Easy Shrimp Ceviche 294

Bacon Cheddar Deviled Eggs 295

Pizza Sticks 3 Ways 297

Rainbow Kettle Corn 302

Factors That May Impact Bipolar Health 305

Sleep 306

Stress 308

Exercise 309

Suggestions for incorporating lifestyle changes to support bipolar health 311

1 Understanding Bipolar Disorder

Manic-depressive disease, or bipolar disorder, is a mental health condition characterized by extreme fluctuations in a person's mood, energy, activity level, and ability to carry out daily tasks. Mania (a state of raised or euphoric mood) and depression (a state of low or sorrowful mood) are two extreme states that people with bipolar illness may experience. Extreme periods of depression might persist for a few days, a few weeks, or even a few months.

Bipolar I, Bipolar II, Cyclothymic illness, and Other Specified and Unspecified Bipolar and Related Disorders are only a few of the many subtypes of bipolar illness. Manic episodes lasting at least a week describe bipolar I illness, while hypomanic episodes and depressive episodes constitute bipolar II disease. At least two years must pass between episodes of hypomania and moderate depression to be diagnosed with cyclothymic disorder.

Uncertain genetic, environmental, and neurological variables are thought to play a role in the development of bipolar illness. Neurotransmitter abnormalities, including those involving dopamine and serotonin, have been linked to bipolar illness in several studies.

Depending on the individual and the nature of the episode, people with bipolar illness may have any number of the following symptoms:

Symptoms of a manic or hypomanic episode include an abnormally high or irritated mood, unusually high levels of energy or activity, a decreased need for sleep, rapid thinking, a lot of chatter, a willingness to take risks, and an inflated feeling of self-worth.

Feelings of sorrow, despair, or emptiness; lack of interest in formerly pleasurable activities; changes in food or sleep; weariness; problems focusing; and/or suicidal or self-harming ideas all constitute a depressive episode.

A mental health practitioner must conduct a series of tests, from a review of symptoms and medical history to a series of psychological and physical examinations, to arrive at a diagnosis of bipolar disorder. Medication, psychotherapy, and behavioral modifications are all potential components of a treatment plan for bipolar illness. Mood stabilizers, antipsychotics, and antidepressants are some of the medications used to treat bipolar disorder.

Individuals with bipolar illness can benefit from psychotherapy like cognitive-behavioral therapy (CBT) and interpersonal therapy (IPT) in order to increase their knowledge of the disorder and their ability to cope with its symptoms. Changing one's lifestyle, like getting adequate sleep, exercising regularly, and eating well, might also help alleviate symptoms.

It's crucial to get aid and support when dealing with bipolar disorder, as it may make daily life difficult. Emotional support can be provided by loved ones, and other useful tools include peer networks and support groups. It's crucial to consult with a mental health expert to create a personalized treatment plan and monitor symptoms closely in order to avoid recurrence.

Overall, bipolar illness is a complicated and often debilitating condition, but it is possible to control symptoms and live a full life with the right therapy and support.

Prevalence and impact of bipolar disorder

About 1%-2% of the world's population suffers from bipolar disorder, a serious mental illness. Mania, hypomania (a milder type of mania), and depression are all symptoms of this long-term mental disorder. These mood episodes can linger for weeks or months and have a devastating effect on a person's ability to go about their everyday life, their relationships, and their general happiness.

Although bipolar disorder can manifest at any age, it often emerges in late adolescence or early adulthood. There is currently no treatment for the illness, and it affects both men and women equally. However, many people with bipolar illness are able to lead full and productive lives with the help of treatment and management.

Bipolar disease may have serious consequences for those who suffer from it as well as their loved ones. Mania and hypomania are extreme states of euphoria and irritability experienced by some people with bipolar illness. Even if these symptoms are originally perceived as beneficial, they often lead to undesirable outcomes including increased risk-taking, financial stress, interpersonal tensions, and performance challenges at work.

Low mood, apathy for once-enjoyed hobbies, inability to focus, and changes in eating and sleeping habits are just some of the symptoms that can arise during depressive episodes in people with bipolar illness. These symptoms can impair one's ability to carry out everyday tasks and may contribute to a sense of futility or unimportance.

The possibility of suicide is one of the many dire outcomes of untreated bipolar illness. However, many people with bipolar illness are able to achieve symptom remission and lead productive lives with the help of therapy and management.

Medication alone is rarely effective in treating bipolar illness, hence psychotherapy is often used in tandem with medication. Mood stabilizers, antipsychotics, and antidepressants are all used to treat bipolar disorder. Symptoms can be lessened and coping abilities enhanced with the use of psychotherapy methods like cognitive-behavioral therapy.

Overall, bipolar disorder is a serious mental illness that affects the lives of many people in profound ways. However, many people with bipolar illness are able to lead full and productive lives with the help of therapy and management. Those who feel they may be suffering from bipolar illness should get evaluated and treated as soon as possible.

Types of bipolar disorder

The mental health disease known as bipolar disorder is marked by extreme shifts in mood as well as energy and activity levels. Different forms of bipolar disease have their own set of signs and treatments. The most common forms of bipolar disorder are as follows:

- Manic episodes, or periods of elevated or irritated mood lasting at least a week, typically accompanied by symptoms like grandiosity, decreased need for sleep, and increased energy and activity, are diagnostic of Bipolar I Disorder. Depressive episodes are a possible symptom of bipolar I disorder.

- Hypomania, a milder form of mania that lasts for at least four days, and at least one major depressive episode are diagnostic criteria for Bipolar II Disorder. Elevated mood, enhanced energy, and increased activity are hallmarks of hypomanic episodes.

- The bipolar illness known as cyclothymia is characterized by phases of hypomania and moderate depression that endure for at least two years in adults and one year in children and adolescents.

- Rapid-Cycling Bipolar Disorder: This type of bipolar disorder is characterized by the presence of four or more mood episodes within a 12-month period. Any of the various forms of bipolar illness can exhibit rapid cycling.

- Mixed Features Bipolar Disorder: This type of bipolar disorder is characterized by the presence of both manic or hypomanic symptoms and depressive symptoms at the same time. Any of the bipolar disorder subtypes might exhibit mixed traits.

- Substance/drug-induced bipolar and related disorder (SMBD) is a subtype of bipolar disorder in which manic or depressive episodes are precipitated by, and subsequently treated with, the introduction or discontinuation of a substance or medicine.

It's crucial to remember that not everyone with bipolar illness fits neatly into one of these categories, as the condition can manifest differently in various people. Mental health professionals are trained to recognize the signs and symptoms of bipolar illness and work with patients to create a personalized treatment plan.

Symptoms and Diagnosis of Bipolar Disorder

Manic depression has been replaced by the more accurate term bipolar disorder, which is a mental illness that causes extreme swings in mood and energy levels. Mania, hypomania, and despair, interspersed with periods of normal mood, are the hallmarks of bipolar disorder. Common signs of bipolar disorder include:

- A manic or hypomanic episode can cause a person with bipolar illness to exhibit symptoms such as a heightened or irritated mood, increased activity, decreased need for sleep, rapid thinking, inflated ideas, impulsivity, and even risk-taking behavior. Hallucinations and delusions are also possible, albeit not as often.

- Depressive Episodes: A person with bipolar illness may feel unhappy, hopeless, worthless, and guilty when experiencing a depressive episode. Difficulties with attention, sleep, and appetite are also possible. They may feel drained of vitality and lose interest in formerly pleasurable activities. During a depressed episode, one may have suicidal ideation or actions.

- A person with bipolar illness may have both manic and depressed symptoms at the same time, a phenomenon known as a mixed episode. This is referred to as a mixed episode and can be quite difficult to handle.

- The term "rapid cycling" refers to a pattern of mood swings in which at least four episodes occur during a 12-month period. Rapid cycling is a feature of some persons with bipolar illness and can make the condition more challenging to treat.

- Irritability, anxiety, agitation, restlessness, racing thoughts, disturbed sleep, and changes in eating and weight are some of the other symptoms that may accompany bipolar illness.

It's crucial to remember that not everyone with bipolar illness may experience all of these symptoms, and that the degree and frequency with which they occur can vary greatly from person to person. You or a loved one should visit a mental health professional if you or they are exhibiting signs of bipolar illness.

Diagnostic criteria for bipolar disorder

Manic-depressive symptom cycles are characteristic of the mental health disease known as bipolar disorder. Because of the severity and disruption these episodes can cause in everyday life, diagnosis and therapy are crucial for symptom management and enhancement of quality of life. According to the DSM-5 (Diagnostic and Statistical Manual of Mental Disorders, Fifth Edition), the following symptoms characterize bipolar disorder:

1. One or more episodes of mania: A manic episode is characterized by an elevated, expansive, or irritated mood for at least a week (or shorter if hospitalization is necessary). During this time, the affected person shows signs of experiencing three or more of the following:
   - Exaggerated sense of importance or pride
   - Reduced sleep need
   - An increase in chattiness or compulsion to continue chitchat
   - A mental sprint or a flight of ideas
   - Distractibility
   - Psychomotor or goal-directed activity increases

2. Participation in enjoyable activities to an unhealthy degree that can lead to negative repercussions (such as wasteful spending, sexual misconduct, or substance misuse).

   - Depression, with at least one significant episode present: For at least two weeks, a person must feel persistent and generalized depression or a lack of interest or pleasure in virtually all activities in order to be diagnosed with a severe depressive episode. More than five of the following symptoms may also be present:
   - Negative emotions for much of the day, on a daily basis
   - Decreased enthusiasm for or enjoyment of previous hobbies
   - Substantial changes in body weight
   - Sleeplessness or oversleeping
   - Psychomotor restlessness or slowing
   - Energy depletion or exhaustion
   - Negative emotions, such as self-loathing or excessive guilt
   - Inability to focus or make a choice
   - Persistent suicidal ideation

3. There is no better explanation for the manic or depressed episode than some other mental health issue or substance addiction.

4. Schizoaffective disorder, schizophrenia, schizophreniform disorder, delusional disorder, and other identified and nonspecific schizophrenia spectrum and other psychotic diseases must not provide a more plausible explanation for the occurrence of the manic and depressed episodes.

As a complicated ailment, bipolar disorder can manifest itself in a variety of ways from person to person. A skilled mental health practitioner should make a diagnosis after carefully considering the patient's symptoms, medical history, and family history. Medication, psychotherapy, and behavioral modifications frequently work together to effectively treat bipolar illness.

Causes and Risk Factors

Extreme ups and downs in mood, known as mania and depression, are hallmarks of the mental health disease known as bipolar disorder. While researchers continue to search for a definitive explanation, they have identified a number of potential risk factors for the onset of bipolar illness. Possible triggers for manic-depressive episodes include:

- Bipolar disorder has been shown to have a hereditary component since it has a strong family recurrence pattern. Several genes have been linked to bipolar illness, while it is probable that several genes have a role.

- Neurotransmitter imbalances are hypothesized to have a role in bipolar illness. Neurotransmitters are chemical messengers in the brain that play a role in regulating mood, behavior, and mental processes. Specifically, it has been suggested that imbalances in the neurotransmitters norepinephrine, dopamine, and serotonin may have a role in the development of bipolar illness.

- Factors in one's environment, such as stress, trauma, or substance addiction, might set off manic episodes in those who are genetically prone to the illness. Bipolar illness may also be triggered by being exposed to certain chemicals or viruses.

- Bipolar disorder has been associated to a number of medical diseases, including thyroid problems, multiple sclerosis, and Parkinson's disease. Mood swings and other bipolar symptoms might be triggered by some of the drugs used to treat these diseases.

- Bipolar illness may be more prone to develop in those who have a history of drug misuse or other mental health issues, or who endured severe stress or trauma as children.

Because of the illness's complexity, it's unlikely that any one thing is solely responsible for someone developing bipolar disorder. Rather, it is believed that bipolar illness is caused by a mix of genetic, environmental, developmental, and chemical abnormalities in the brain. Getting a proper diagnosis and treatment for bipolar illness requires the assistance of a trained mental health expert.

Genetic factors

The psychiatric condition known as bipolar disorder is complicated, with both hereditary and environmental variables playing a role in its development. There is still much we don't know about the genetics of bipolar illness, but researchers have pinpointed a number of genes as possible risk factors.

The CACNA1C gene, which codes for a calcium channel protein involved in the control of neuronal signaling, is one of the most investigated genes in bipolar illness. The chance of developing bipolar disorder, as well as schizophrenia and significant depression, has been linked to variations in this gene.

The ANK3 gene, which is involved in neural signaling, has also been linked to an elevated risk of bipolar disorder as well as other mental disorders. Similarly, mutations in the BDNF gene—which encodes a protein critical for brain development and survival—have been linked to an increased chance of developing bipolar illness.

Several genetic variables, including family history of the condition and certain chromosomal abnormalities, have been identified as possible risk factors for bipolar disorder in addition to particular genes.

Even though some people may be predisposed to developing bipolar illness due to hereditary factors, this is not always the case. Stress, substance misuse, and traumatic experiences are all environmental variables that have been linked to the emergence of bipolar illness.

Furthermore, several genes and gene-environment interactions may be involved in the complicated link between genetics and bipolar disease. Since the findings of genetic testing for bipolar disorder are not likely to offer conclusive answers regarding an individual's risk for the condition, the testing is not currently suggested.

Although genetics do play a part in the onset of bipolar illness, environmental variables also play a significant role in the development of this complicated condition. The development of efficient treatments and therapies for people with bipolar illness can be aided by a better understanding of these characteristics.

Environmental factors

The mental health illness known as bipolar disorder is complicated, with several contributing elements including genetics, biology, and the environment. Researchers have shown that environmental variables may contribute to the onset and progression of bipolar disease, although the specific reason is still unknown.

Some of the environmental risk factors for bipolar disorder are as follows:

- Episodes of bipolar illness can be triggered by stress, including issues in interpersonal relationships, financial hardships, and pressures at work. Additionally, stress can exacerbate symptoms and make treatment more challenging.

- Substance abuse: Abuse of drugs or alcohol can bring on or exacerbate bipolar symptoms. Substance misuse also raises the suicide risk and can disrupt the effectiveness of treatment.

- Sleep difficulties, such as insomnia or oversleeping, can either initiate or exacerbate bipolar symptoms. Disrupted sleep has been linked to negative effects on medication management and mental health.

- Some persons with bipolar illness find that the shift from summer to fall, in particular, brings on an episode. As the days get shorter and darker, some people experience depression known as seasonal affective disorder.

- Toxins: Heavy metals, herbicides, and industrial chemicals may all raise the risk of bipolar disorder when exposed to large enough doses. Exposure to air pollution has been linked to an increased risk of mental disorders, according to the literature.

- These external influences may have a role in the onset and progression of bipolar illness, but they are not responsible for the disorder on their own. There are other biological aspects at play, such as genetics, brain anatomy, and function.

It is safe to say, elements in one's environment, such as stress, substance misuse, sleep difficulties, seasonal changes, and exposure to toxins, might have an impact on the onset and progression of bipolar illness. Together, medication and treatment can help persons with bipolar illness improve their outcomes by managing these characteristics.

Brain chemistry and structure

Manic episodes (extreme elation and vigor) and depressive episodes (sadness, despair, and a lack of interest) are hallmarks of the mental health disease known as bipolar disorder. It is unclear what triggers bipolar illness, although studies point to a combination of hereditary and environmental causes.

The connection between bipolar illness and changes in brain chemistry and structure is one area that has received much attention. Neurotransmitters are chemical messengers in the brain, and it is theorized that alterations in their levels may play a role in the emergence of bipolar illness.

Studies have linked an imbalance in neurotransmitters including dopamine, serotonin, and norepinephrine to the development of bipolar illness. While serotonin and norepinephrine regulate mood, hunger, and sleep, dopamine is involved in motivation, reward, and pleasure.

Imaging studies have also demonstrated that the prefrontal cortex, amygdala, and hippocampus of people with bipolar disorder may be different in form and function. Controlling emotions, making choices, and remembering are all functions of these specific brain areas.

Changes in brain chemistry and structure are thought to contribute to the symptoms of bipolar illness, however the exact link between the two is not well known. A reduction in serotonin activity during depressive episodes may contribute to emotions of despair and hopelessness, whereas an increase in dopamine activity during manic episodes may contribute to the overwhelming enthusiasm and energy experienced during these periods.

Treatment for bipolar illness often consists of a mix of medication and therapy, both of which can enhance mood control by modulating neurotransmitter activity. Mood-stabilizing drugs, antidepressants, and antipsychotics may be prescribed, and therapy can aid in the development of coping mechanisms and the improvement of emotional regulation.

Although bipolar illness may be linked to alterations in brain chemistry and structure, it is crucial to remember that there are many other factors at play. The most effective treatments typically take a multifaceted approach, focusing on the patient's physical and mental health simultaneously.

Risk Factors for Bipolar Disorder

The precise reason why some people develop bipolar illness is still unknown, researchers have found a number of potential contributors.

Several genes have been linked to the development of bipolar illness, and studies have shown that the ailment tends to run in families. The likelihood of acquiring bipolar disorder is higher if you have a close family who suffers from the disease.

Brain imaging studies have demonstrated that persons with bipolar disorder have atypical brain anatomy and function. Mood swings and other symptoms may be exacerbated by these variations.

- Substance abuse: Abuse of stimulants like cocaine and amphetamines, in particular, can set off mania in those who suffer from bipolar illness. Use of alcoholic beverages or marijuana might potentially exacerbate symptoms and make therapy less effective.

- Manic or depressed episodes in persons with bipolar illness can be triggered by stressful life events like the death of a loved one or the loss of a job.

- A higher chance of having bipolar illness has been linked to a number of medical ailments, including thyroid problems, MS, and Parkinson's disease.

- Manic episodes in patients with bipolar illness can be triggered by changes in sleep schedules or a lack of sleep.

- The chance of having bipolar illness later in life is higher in those who had traumatic events as children, such as physical or sexual abuse.

Having these risk factors does not ensure that a person will acquire bipolar disorder, but it does increase the likelihood that they will. The illness is multifaceted, affected by both hereditary and environmental factors, among others. However, being aware of these aspects can aid in the recognition of any warning signals and the subsequent pursuit of therapy.

2. The Bipolar Treatment Options

A person's mood, energy, and capacity to perform can all be negatively impacted by bipolar illness. Mania or hypomania alternate with periods of depression. Medication and psychotherapy are often used together to treat bipolar illness. Some of the available treatments for bipolar disorder are as follows:

- Medication: Mood stabilizers, antipsychotics, and antidepressants are just some of the medications that can be used to treat bipolar illness. Treatment for bipolar illness often begins with mood stabilizers such lithium, valproic acid, or carbamazepine. Bipolar disorder, which can include periods of mania or hypomania, can be treated with antipsychotics such olanzapine, risperidone, and quetiapine. In treating depressive episodes, antidepressants may be used judiciously in conjunction with mood stabilizers.

- People with bipolar illness may benefit from psychotherapy, often known as talk therapy. Bipolar disorder treatment options include cognitive behavioral therapy (CBT) and interpersonal therapy (IPT). Mood episodes can be mitigated with CBT by recognizing and altering the unpleasant thoughts and actions that lead to them. The primary goals of IPT are conflict resolution and relational enhancement.

- Electroshock treatment, or ECT: The goal of electroconvulsive therapy (ECT) is to induce a seizure in a patient under medical supervision. People with bipolar illness who have not responded to other therapies may be offered this as a last option. Electroconvulsive therapy (ECT) has shown useful in the treatment of manic and depressive episodes, but it is not without risk.

- Modifications to One's Way of Life: Alterations in way of life can be useful in the management of manic-depressive illness. Some examples are working out frequently, eating right, sleeping enough, not abusing drugs or alcohol, and finding healthy ways to deal with stress like yoga and meditation.

An individual with bipolar illness should consult a mental health expert to determine the best course of therapy. As symptoms evolve and new medicines are developed, it may be necessary to modify an initial course of treatment. People who have bipolar illness can recover and live satisfying lives if they get the help they need.

Medication

Medication and talk therapy are often used together to treat bipolar disorder, a mental health disease. Mood-stabilizing medications have been shown to lessen symptoms and protect against recurrence. Medication for bipolar disorder often includes the following:

- Mood stabilizers including lithium, valproic acid, and carbamazepine are the mainstays of treatment for bipolar disorder. These drugs are effective at lowering manic and depressive episodes and decreasing mood swings.

- Mood stabilizers and antipsychotics, such risperidone and olanzapine, are a common treatment for bipolar illness. Mania and psychosis symptoms may be mitigated using these drugs.

- Bipolar depression may be treated with antidepressants such selective serotonin reuptake inhibitors (SSRIs). These drugs are often taken with care and in conjunction with a mood stabilizer since they can cause mania in some persons with bipolar illness.

- Benzodiazepines and other anti-anxiety drugs may help with the anxiety that typically comes along with bipolar illness. It's important to use caution when using these drugs because of the risk of addiction.

It's crucial to remember that different people respond differently to different drugs when it comes to managing their bipolar disease. Working closely with a mental health expert to monitor symptoms and change therapy as required is essential while searching for the proper medicine or combination of medications.

Treatment for bipolar illness often include a combination of medication and psychotherapy. Psychotherapies such as cognitive behavioral therapy (CBT), family focused therapy (FFT), and interpersonal and social rhythm therapy (IPSRT) have been shown to be effective in the treatment of mental health issues.

As a last thought, it is important to note that mood stabilizers are often the first line of therapy for bipolar illness when it comes to medication. Depending on the patient's symptoms and needs, mood stabilizers may be combined with other medicines, such as antipsychotics, antidepressants, or anti-anxiety drugs. It may take time and the help of a mental health expert to find the proper prescription or combination of medications.

Psychotherapy

When combined with medication, psychotherapy can be an effective treatment for bipolar illness.

The psychotherapeutic approach known as cognitive-behavioral therapy (CBT) has shown promise in the management of bipolar illness. The goal of cognitive behavioral therapy (CBT), a form of talk therapy, in the treatment of mood swings is to help patients recognize and replace harmful thinking and behavior patterns.

During cognitive behavioral therapy (CBT) for bipolar illness, the therapist and patient work together to determine what sets off the patient's mood swings and then devise techniques to counteract them. The therapist may also encourage the patient to establish a regimen that includes good behaviors like sufficient rest, physical activity, and nutritious food.

Interpersonal and social rhythm therapy (IPSRT) is another form of psychotherapy that has shown promise for those with bipolar illness. When trying to regulate one's mood, IPSRT emphasizes sticking to normal daily habits including eating and sleeping at set times. The value of having and keeping up positive connections is emphasized in IPSRT as a means of lowering stress and enhancing well-being.

Individuals with bipolar illness may also benefit from supportive therapy in addition to the aforementioned methods of treatment. During supportive therapy, you and your therapist will talk about your symptoms, their impact on your life, and how you may best manage them.

Psychotherapy, when combined with other forms of care, can be beneficial for some people with bipolar illness. It can aid people in learning to recognize the signs of a mood episode, creating a plan to deal with those triggers, sticking to those routines, and surrounding themselves with positive people. It's best to consult with a medical professional to figure out which form of psychotherapy would work best for you.

Lifestyle changes

Lifestyle adjustments, in addition to medication, can be helpful in controlling the symptoms of bipolar illness. People with bipolar disorder may benefit from the following lifestyle adjustments:

- Get into a Schedule: Establishing a pattern can assist maintain positive emotions and improve sleep quality. Sleeping and getting up at the same times every day, planning out one's meals and physical activity, and reserving time for one's own care and relaxation are all examples of this.

- Exercising has been demonstrated to increase mood and lessen anxiety and despair. People with bipolar illness might benefit greatly from improved sleep due to regular exercise.

- Supporting brain health and maintaining emotional stability may be achieved by eating a diet that is well-rounded and contains a variety of nutritious foods, lean protein, and healthy fats. If you're having trouble sleeping or regulating your mood, cutting out alcoholic beverages and caffeine may help.

- De-stressing: For many persons with bipolar illness, stress is a major precipitator of manic or depressive episodes. Meditation, yoga, and deep breathing exercises are just a few stress-reduction methods that may be included into a person's daily routine to help them feel calmer and more relaxed.

- Having a solid social network in place can aid those with bipolar illness in controlling their symptoms and enhancing their quality of life. Mental health specialists, as well as friends and family, might be helpful here.

- In order to better manage their mood fluctuations, persons with bipolar illness might benefit from developing a greater awareness of their own thoughts and feelings via mindfulness practice. Some examples of mindfulness practices are meditation, scanning one's body, and deep breathing.

To sum up, medication is generally essential for controlling bipolar disease, but adjustments in lifestyle can also play a vital role in symptom management. People with bipolar illness might benefit greatly from developing regular routines that include engaging in physical activity, eating a healthy food, reducing stress, seeking and accepting social support, and practicing mindfulness. A mental health expert should be consulted to create a treatment plan that takes into account both medication and behavioral modifications.

3. Living with Bipolar Disorder

People with bipolar disorder experience strong highs (mania or hypomania) and lows (depression) in their moods. Having bipolar illness can be difficult to live with, but it is manageable with the right therapy and support. Methods for coping with bipolar disorder are as follows:

- Get in touch with a specialist: An appropriate diagnosis and treatment plan can only be determined in conjunction with a trained mental health practitioner. Medication, psychotherapy, or a mix of the two is often used in treatment. Never give up if it takes some time to discover a treatment plan that works for you; there is excellent help out there.

- Find out more about the illness: The ability to control symptoms and effectively communicate with your healthcare team and loved ones is greatly enhanced by an awareness of bipolar illness and its effects. Learn to recognize the early symptoms of mood swings and create a strategy to control them.

- Establish a regular schedule: Developing a regular schedule might help you maintain a steady disposition and avoid emotional ups and downs. Make it a priority to get enough shut-eye, go the gym frequently, and eat right.

- Set up a backbone: Having a strong network of loved ones and medical experts at your side may make a world of difference when dealing with bipolar disease. The emotional and social support of a group of people who understand your situation may be invaluable.

- Mood swings can be caused by stress, therefore it's important to learn to control your reaction to stressful situations. Stress and anxiety can be mitigated via the practice of relaxation techniques like deep breathing, meditation, or yoga.

- Maintain a vigilance in the administration of medications: Managing bipolar illness requires strict adherence to prescribed medication. Develop a drug management strategy that works for you and your healthcare practitioner, and be sure to mention any unwanted effects or concerns right away.

Bipolar illness is difficult to manage without therapy and support, but both may make daily life easier. Bipolar illness may be managed and quality of life improved by several means, including getting professional treatment, learning about the disease, adopting a daily routine, constructing a support system, controlling stress, and remaining careful about medication administration.

Coping strategies

Individuals with bipolar illness can learn to control their symptoms with medication and self-care and go on to have productive lives. Some methods of managing bipolar disorder are as follows:

- Medication: Medications including antidepressants, antipsychotics, and mood stabilizers are commonly used to treat bipolar disorder. It's crucial to collaborate closely with a healthcare professional in order to identify the medicine (or combination of medications) that will be most effective for each patient.

- Treatment through talk therapy may be useful in coping with bipolar illness. Individuals can develop coping mechanisms, stress management strategies, and better family communication through cognitive-behavioral therapy (CBT), psychoeducation, and family therapy.

- Modifying your way of living in a healthy way can also aid in the management of bipolar illness. Symptoms may subside if one engages in regular physical activity, eats a nutritious diet, reduces stress, and abstains from using drugs and alcohol.

- Having reliable people around you might be helpful while dealing with bipolar disorder. Emotional support can be found from friends and family, and those with similar circumstances can find community through support groups.

- Self-care is an integral part of bipolar illness management. Individuals may better manage stress and boost their mood by partaking in activities that bring them joy and relaxation, including reading, listening to music, or taking a warm bath.

- It may be helpful for people with bipolar illness to think forward to times when their mood is likely to be more unstable, such as when they are experiencing stress or big life changes. It might be helpful to have a strategy in place for dealing with symptoms at these times.

Patients with bipolar illness should collaborate closely with their healthcare team to create a personalized treatment strategy. People with bipolar illness can learn to control their symptoms and lead productive lives with the help of therapy and self-care.

Managing relationships

Relationship management is tough for everyone, but those with bipolar illness may find it especially so. Extreme mood fluctuations, from great energy and joy to severe melancholy, are a hallmark of the mental health disease known as bipolar disorder. Relationships with loved ones, friends, and romantic partners may be especially challenging for those with bipolar illness due to the disruptive nature of their mood swings. Relationship management can be challenging for those with bipolar disorder, but it is possible with the correct tools and support.

Here are some suggestions for coping with interpersonal connections while coping with bipolar disorder:

- Talk things out: It's crucial to be honest with the people close to you about your bipolar condition. Tell them how you feel and ask what they can do to help. Relationships are strengthened and mutual support is increased when people are open and honest with one another.

- Follow your treatment plan to the letter, including taking your medicine on time and showing up for your therapy appointments. This can aid in symptom management and the avoidance of relationship-damaging mood swings.

- Find the causes: Figure out what stresses, sleep deprivation, or meals put you in a bad mood. You may take measures to prevent or deal with these triggers if you are aware of them.

- Self-care is essential in dealing with bipolar disease and keeping relationships stable. Among these include maintaining a regular exercise routine, eating a balanced diet, and getting plenty of sleep.

- Boundaries should be established in all relationships, but notably those involving one's emotional well-being. Make it clear to others what you will and will not tolerate. Conflicts can be avoided and stress levels lowered as a result.

- Find help: Maintaining a good social life and coping with bipolar disease both need a strong support network. A therapist, group of friends, or relative can all help.

- Learn the facts: Find out as much as you can about bipolar illness, from possible origins and treatments to possible symptoms. You can learn more about your illness and express yourself clearly to others if you do this.

Having bipolar disease makes it more difficult to maintain relationships, but it is doable with proper resources and support. You may have healthy and satisfying relationships with the people in your life if you are honest with one another, follow your treatment plan, recognize your triggers, engage in self-care, establish appropriate boundaries, seek help when you need it, and educate yourself.

Career considerations for people with bipolar disorder

People with bipolar illness may face some unusual difficulties in the job, but with the right treatment and assistance, they can achieve professional success. Some career tips for those with bipolar disorder are as follows.

- When seeking concessions and understanding from one's employer and coworkers, some people with bipolar illness prefer to come clean about their condition. The stigma that still exists around mental health issues makes this a tough choice to make, but doing so can aid in getting the necessary adjustments done.

- Alternative work schedules: People with bipolar illness, who may suffer mood episodes that make it challenging to function in an office setting, may benefit from flexible work arrangements, such as working from home or having a flexible schedule.

- Mood episodes in persons with bipolar illness are often triggered by stress, therefore learning to effectively handle stress is essential. Time management, setting priorities, and pausing to recharge are all examples.

- Treatment of bipolar illness requires strict adherence to prescribed medication. Working with a healthcare practitioner to make dose adjustments or switch drugs can help reduce unwanted effects.

- Having a strong social support system of family, friends, and coworkers can be beneficial in managing the symptoms of bipolar disease. Some ways to do this are to chat freely with trustworthy coworkers, join support groups, or join online communities.

- Planning a career involves thinking about the demands of a job and whether or not they can be met by someone with bipolar illness. Career-wise, this might mean reevaluating aspirations or looking for a different line of work that better suits their skills and interests.

- Taking care of yourself is crucial while coping with the effects of bipolar illness. Physical activity, nutritious nutrition, adequate rest, and the pursuit of enjoyable pursuits are all examples of ways to take care of oneself.

People with bipolar illness should also collaborate with mental health specialists and reach out for help from their workplace and peers when they need it. Successful and satisfying professions are possible for persons with bipolar illness who get treatment and support.

Stigma and Misconceptions for people with bipolar disorder

Stigma and misunderstandings around bipolar disease continue to be important obstacles for those who live with the condition, despite the frequency of bipolar disorder and the increased awareness of mental health concerns in general. People with bipolar disorder may face discrimination and misinformation, including but not limited to the following:

- Personality flaws are at the root of bipolar disorder: The false belief that bipolar illness is caused by a lack of moral fiber is one of the most pervasive and damaging myths surrounding the condition. This misconception can lead to feelings of guilt and shame, which in turn can discourage people with bipolar illness from getting help.

- Aggression is a common symptom of bipolar disorder. People with bipolar disorder are often misunderstood and assumed to be more prone to aggressive or violent behavior. The great majority of people with bipolar illness, however, are not violent and are no more prone to engage in violent conduct than people without the disease, as has been demonstrated by several studies.

- Some people with bipolar disease really are "crazy" One such false belief about people with bipolar disease is that they are "crazy" or "unpredictable." This misconception may be hurtful and isolating, since it discourages people with bipolar illness from reaching out for help and sharing their stories.

- Contrary to popular belief, medication is not a "quick fix" for bipolar illness and may not be effective for all people with the condition. Recognizing that bipolar disorder is a long-term condition that needs constant care and attention is crucial.

- Successful living is impossible for those with bipolar disorder: If a person with bipolar disorder is already feeling dismal or despair, this misperception might make their situation even worse. However, many people with bipolar illness may have meaningful and successful lives with the help of treatment and support.

As a result of these beliefs and stigmas, people with bipolar illness may experience negative outcomes such as elevated levels of shame, isolation, and hopelessness. It is crucial to dispel these false beliefs and encourage a more nuanced and sympathetic knowledge of bipolar disease. This may involve campaigning for better access to mental health treatment and support, spreading awareness of the disorder, and sharing stories of people who have successfully managed the condition.

Common myths about bipolar disorder

Mood and energy fluctuations are only two symptoms of bipolar disorder, a complicated mental health disease that can be difficult to manage. Getting the proper treatment and support for bipolar illness can be challenging due to widespread beliefs and misunderstandings regarding the condition. Some misconceptions that circulate concerning bipolar disorder are as follows:

- Bipolar disorder is not merely mood swings, that's a myth.

A person with bipolar illness may have mood swings, but they are not the same as "normal" mood swings. A person's life, relationships, and capacity to function can all be severely impacted by bipolar illness, making it a very serious mental health disease.

- Bipolar individuals never experience anything except extreme highs and lows is a common misconception.

The severity of manic or depressive episodes, as well as the frequency with which they occur, and the presence or absence of stable mood between episodes, all vary greatly among those with bipolar illness.

- The misconception that bipolar illness mainly affects adults.

Bipolar disorder is equally common in young people and adolescents. Some patients with bipolar illness may actually show their initial symptoms while still a kid or a teenager.

- Those who suffer from bipolar illness are only "crazy" or "unstable."

True sufferers of bipolar disease are neither insane nor unbalanced. They suffer from a medical condition that lowers their emotional and physical reserves, yet with help they may live happy, productive lives.

- There is no effective treatment for bipolar disorder.

The truth is that bipolar illness may be treated. Medication, counseling, and behavioral modifications are all viable options. Most people with bipolar illness may find effective therapy that improves their symptoms and quality of life, but it may take some time.

Educating the public on the facts of bipolar disease and debunking these misunderstandings is crucial. By learning more about this issue, we can lessen the stigma associated with it and better assist those who have it.

Reducing stigma and improving understanding

Promoting mental health and wellness includes lowering the stigma associated with bipolar illness and increasing public knowledge of the condition. Some suggestions for easing prejudice and expanding comprehension:

Myths and misconceptions regarding bipolar disorder can be dispelled via awareness and education efforts. Educating the public about the condition, its symptoms, and the options for treatment can do a lot to break down the stigma associated with it.

The way people with bipolar illness are viewed can be greatly affected by the terminology used to discuss mental health issues. Language that puts the focus on the individual, rather than the condition, such as "person with bipolar disorder" rather than "bipolar person," can be useful in combating prejudice and increasing acceptance.

Open discourse about bipolar disease has been shown to be effective in reducing stigma and increasing knowledge of the condition. This can be done through the provision of support groups or treatment, the promotion of open and honest talks about mental health, or the creation of safe spaces in which people with bipolar illness can share their experiences.

The stigma associated with bipolar illness can be lessened and the public's awareness of the condition can be improved by challenging misconceptions and inaccurate depictions of the disorder in the media and popular culture. Advocating for more sympathetic and realistic portrayals of people with bipolar illness in the media is one way to help.

Funding research into bipolar illness can help us learn more about the condition and find better ways to treat it. This might include taking part in clinical trials or lobbying for more money to be allocated to studies of mental health.

In order to lessen the stigma associated with bipolar illness and increase the likelihood of positive results, it is important to encourage people with the disease to seek treatment. This may be done in a number of ways, including making therapy more easily accessible and fostering an environment where people with mental health issues are accepted and supported.

Better mental health outcomes for everyone can be achieved by working to eliminate discrimination and increase public awareness about bipolar illness.

Future Research and Directions

Research into the origins and treatments of bipolar disorder must continue in order to further our understanding of this complicated illness. Here are some potential areas of study and new treatment options for bipolar disorder:

Researchers are still trying to pin down the exact roles played by biological and genetic elements in the onset and course of bipolar illness. New therapies for bipolar illness may be developed in light of the possibility that advances in genetic research may reveal the precise genes that enhance susceptibility to the condition.

There is growing interest in creating individualized treatments for bipolar disease that take into account each patient's specific set of symptoms, genetic composition, and pharmacological response. Better, more specific therapies for bipolar illness may become available as precision medicine develops.

Use of smartphone applications and online psychotherapy are examples of digital and mobile health therapies that are fast becoming a focus of study in the field of bipolar illness. Medication adherence, symptom monitoring, and post-clinic visit support are three areas where these interventions might be most helpful.

Several novel pharmacological therapies, including as ketamine, N-acetylcysteine, and omega-3 fatty acids, are now under study for the treatment of bipolar illness. These therapies have the potential to ameliorate mood instability and lessen the intensity of mood swings.

Exercise, mindfulness, and good sleep hygiene are just a few examples of the kinds of behavioral and lifestyle therapies that are gaining popularity as potential treatments for bipolar illness. These measures have the potential to enhance mood stability and lessen the likelihood of mood episodes.

Comorbid conditions: Anxiety and drug use disorders are common companions of bipolar disorder. In the future, scientists should work to create holistic treatments that tackle both bipolar illness and its co-occurring diseases.

Additional study is required to identify the specific biochemical and genetic characteristics that predispose individuals to bipolar illness, to create more individualized treatment approaches, and to explore new therapies including digital interventions and innovative pharmaceutical treatments. Improving outcomes for people with bipolar illness may also require further study into the treatment of comorbid disorders and the influence of lifestyle choices.

4. Bipolar Disorder and its Impact on Diet

Manic episodes (times of great energy, exhilaration, and impulsivity) and depressive episodes (times of low energy, sadness, and hopelessness) are two of the most prominent symptoms of bipolar illness.

Appetite and food preferences can be significantly impacted by bipolar illness due to mood swings and adverse effects of medications. Some dietary influences of bipolar disorder are listed below.

Changes in appetite: Some persons with bipolar illness report increased hunger and a desire for sweet or fatty meals during manic episodes. However, hunger might diminish during depressed periods, leading to a loss of interest in eating or even inadvertent weight loss.

Side effects of drugs used to treat bipolar illness include changes in appetite and gastrointestinal function. Some drugs can enhance or reduce appetite, while others might cause nausea and vomiting.

Manic and depressed episodes can make it difficult for people with bipolar illness to eat normally, increasing the risk of vitamin shortages. Vitamin D, omega-3 fatty acids, and various B vitamins are often deficient in patients with bipolar illness.

Eating disorders: As a coping mechanism for mood swings or medication side effects, some persons with bipolar illness may develop disordered eating behaviors such binge eating or restricted eating.

People with bipolar illness can benefit from a healthy diet that includes a wide range of foods from each major food group. A healthcare physician or certified dietitian may help guide you through the process of creating a diet plan tailored to your specific requirements and interests. In addition to medical treatment, patients with bipolar illness can benefit from self-care practices including stress management and frequent exercise.

Nutrients for Bipolar Health

Genetic and environmental variables both have a role in the development of bipolar disorder. There is mounting evidence that some nutrients may have a role in promoting mental health and lowering the symptoms of bipolar illness, in addition to medication and therapy. Some foods have been demonstrated to improve bipolar disorder symptoms.

Omega-3 fatty acids: These fatty acids, which may be found in salmon, sardines, flaxseeds, walnuts, and other sources, have been demonstrated to have anti-inflammatory properties and to promote brain function. Omega-3 supplementation has been shown to ameliorate manic and depressive symptoms in people with bipolar illness.

Magnesium is an essential element for a number of functions in the body, including muscle and nerve health, and it also has a sedative impact on the nervous system. An increased vulnerability to mood disorders like bipolar has been linked to low magnesium levels. Magnesium supplements may help people with bipolar disorder relax and have a better night's sleep.

Vitamin D: Vitamin D is a vitamin that has been found to have substantial impacts on mood and brain function, in addition to being required for bone health. Mood disorders, such as bipolar illness, have been linked to low vitamin D levels. Vitamin D supplementation has been shown to ameliorate depressive symptoms and boost mood in people with bipolar illness.

B vitamins: B vitamins, such as folate and B12, are crucial to neurotransmitter synthesis and normal brain function. An increased vulnerability to mood disorders like bipolar has been linked to deficiency in certain vitamins. People with bipolar illness who take B vitamin supplements may have fewer depressive episodes and more mental clarity.

Zinc: Zinc is a mineral that has been proven to play a role in both immunological and brain function. Mood disorders, such as bipolar illness, have been linked to low zinc levels. Zinc supplementation has shown promise in enhancing mood and cognition in people with bipolar illness.

Although these nutrients may improve the health of people with bipolar disorder, they are not a replacement for medication or treatment. Before beginning a new supplement or making alterations to one's current diet or pharmaceutical regimen, those who suffer from bipolar illness should consult with their doctor.

Nutrients that support bipolar health, such as omega-3 fatty acids, B vitamins, and magnesium

People with bipolar illness may benefit greatly from proper nutrition. Some nutrients that may be helpful are listed below.

Fatty acids omega-3: Polyunsaturated fats like omega-3 fatty acids are crucial to health in many ways, and that includes brain function. Research suggests that omega-3s, and specifically EPA and DHA, may help regulate mood and lessen the likelihood of manic episodes in those with bipolar illness. Flaxseeds, chia seeds, walnuts, and fatty fish like salmon and mackerel are all excellent sources of omega-3s.

B vitamins: B vitamins, especially vitamin B12 and folate, are crucial for brain function and may be helpful for people with bipolar illness. Neurotransmitters like serotonin and dopamine can't be made without vitamin B12, whereas folate is essential for DNA synthesis and other vital cellular activities. Plant foods, fortified grains, and animal items like eggs and dairy are all excellent places to get your B vitamins.

Magnesium: Magnesium is a vital element that helps with many different biological activities, including nerve impulse transmission and mood stabilization. Researchers have shown that magnesium has promising effects for those with bipolar illness, including a decrease in both the intensity and frequency of mania. Magnesium may be found in abundance in foods including legumes, nuts, seeds, and whole grains.

Vitamin D: Vitamin D is crucial for general health, including mental wellbeing. Supplementation with vitamin D may help with mood control, and research suggests that low levels of vitamin D may be linked to an increased risk of bipolar illness. Fatty fish, fortified dairy products, and sun exposure are all good ways to get your daily dose of vitamin D.

Zinc: Zinc is a vital element that aids in numerous biological processes, including cognition and emotional stability. Studies have indicated that people with bipolar illness may have decreased amounts of zinc, suggesting that supplementation may help regulate mood. Zinc is found in high concentrations in foods including meat, seafood, nuts, and seeds, and whole grains.

Though these nutrients have shown promise in helping some people with bipolar illness, they should not be taken in place of medical care for the condition. Medication, counseling, and behavioral modifications are common components of effective treatment plans for bipolar illness. A healthcare provider or qualified dietitian should be consulted before making any major dietary or supplementation changes.

Foods to Eat on a Bipolar Diet

A bipolar diet is one that has been developed to aid in mental health and the control of manic and depressive episodes associated with bipolar illness. There is no one "bipolar diet," however some foods may help stabilize mood in persons with bipolar illness. Foods that are recommended for those with bipolar disorder include:

- Vegetables and fruits: These food groups are rich in essential elements such vitamins, minerals, and phytonutrients that support physical and mental well-being. In addition, they contain a lot of fiber, which may keep blood sugar levels steady and prevent inflammation.

- Brown rice, quinoa, and whole wheat bread are all examples of whole grains. They are high in fiber and complex carbs, both of which assist to regulate blood sugar and boost your mood.

- Mood-regulating neurotransmitters like serotonin and dopamine are produced in part by the body from the amino acids found in lean protein sources like chicken, fish, and tofu.

- Foods abundant in healthy fats, such as nuts and seeds, can aid in lowering inflammation and bolstering cognitive function. Protein and fiber can be found in them as well.

- Probiotic-rich fermented foods like yogurt, kefir, and sauerkraut are good for your digestive tract and your mood.

- High-omega-3-fat foods: they have been demonstrated to improve mental health. Omega-3s are a form of good fat. Fatty fish like salmon and sardines are good sources of omega-3s, as are flaxseeds, chia seeds, walnuts, and other nuts and seeds.

A bipolar diet should not be considered a replacement for conventional medical care for bipolar disorder. Consult a mental health expert to create a personalized treatment plan that takes into account your specific needs and goals and may involve medication, counselling, and adjustments to your diet.

Foods support brain health and mood regulation

Positive effects on physical and mental health have been linked to a diet rich in whole, natural foods. There is currently no known treatment for bipolar disease, however some foods have been shown to help with mood control and overall brain health. Here are a few illustrations:

- Omega-3 fatty acids, which are abundant in fatty fish like salmon, mackerel, and sardines, have been linked to improved brain function. Studies reveal that omega-3s might aid in mood regulation and are crucial for normal brain function.

- Spinach, kale, and collard greens are just a few examples of the leafy green vegetables that are loaded with nutrients vital to maintaining healthy brain function. They are high in magnesium and folate, both of which have a role in maintaining a healthy mood.

- Complex carbohydrates, found in foods like brown rice, quinoa, and whole-wheat bread, are a reliable supply of fuel for the brain. The B vitamins they contain are crucial to normal nerve and brain activity.

- Chicken, turkey, and tofu are all great examples of lean proteins that can help keep your brain working properly. They are rich in the amino acids needed to make the mood-regulating neurotransmitters.

These items are only the beginning of a nutritious diet that also includes a wide range of fruits, vegetables, whole grains, lean protein, and healthy fats that may help you feel and look your best. Avoiding the harmful effects of consuming too much processed food, sugary drinks, and alcohol is also crucial.

People with bipolar illness can benefit from eating a diet high in nutrient-dense foods since it promotes brain function and helps regulate their moods. Essential nutrients for proper brain function include omega-3 fatty acids, folate, magnesium, the B vitamins, and amino acids. Consuming a wide range of foods that are particularly high in these nutrients can be beneficial to health.

Foods to Avoid on a Bipolar Diet

There is no one "bipolar diet," although some people with the disease may find that particular foods cause or exacerbate their mood swings and other symptoms. As a result, avoiding or reducing consumption of specific foods may prove beneficial for certain people. Some foods to avoid are listed below.

- Foods with a high glycemic index (GI): White bread, spaghetti, and sugary beverages are examples of high-GI meals, which can raise blood sugar levels quickly before causing a dramatic decline. Some people with bipolar illness experience this as irritation and mood swings.

- Caffeine: As a stimulant, caffeine can cause sleep disruption and anxiety, both of which can amplify the negative effects of bipolar illness.

- Alcohol: Because of its potential to cause sleep disruption and irritability, people with bipolar illness should restrict or abstain from alcohol use.

- Fast food, frozen meals, and packaged snacks are all examples of processed foods, and they often include a lot of harmful fats, sugar, and salt, as well as potentially mood-altering preservatives and chemicals.

- Consuming a lot of red meat has been linked to an increased chance of developing bipolar illness, according to some research.

- Omega-6 fatty acids: Omega-6 fatty acids, which are often present in processed meals and some vegetable oils like maize and soybean oil, may increase inflammation in the body and exacerbate symptoms of bipolar illness.

- Gluten sensitivity, which is suspected in some people with bipolar illness, can cause inflammation and exacerbate symptoms. Grains including wheat, barley, and rye contain gluten.

It's worth noting that not everyone with bipolar illness will react negatively to certain foods, and others may be able to eat them without any bad effects at all. However, if a person discovers that a certain meal seems to exacerbate their symptoms, cutting back on or avoiding it altogether may be beneficial. It is also recommended that people with bipolar illness have a diet rich in fruits, vegetables, whole grains, lean protein, and healthy fats. Individuals may get the most out of their nutrition plan by working with their healthcare physician and a certified dietitian.

Foods can contribute to mood instability and inflammation

It's vital for everyone to eat well, but it may be more crucial for those with bipolar illness. meals like processed meals, fizzy beverages, and alcohol may all be harmful to someone with bipolar disorder. Here's a quick rundown of the issues that may arise from consuming certain foods:

Chips, crackers, and other processed snack foods are notorious for their high levels of sugar, salt, and harmful fats and additives. Mood swings and instability may be exacerbated by the quick rise and fall in blood sugar levels caused by eating these meals. Furthermore, the lack of key elements including vitamins and minerals in processed meals can lead to inflammation and other health issues.

Soda, sports drinks, and sweetened coffee beverages are all examples of sugary drinks that are often heavy in sugar and empty calories. Rapid fluctuations in blood sugar levels, brought on by drinking these beverages, have been linked to irritability and mania. High-sugar diets have also been related to inflammation, which can exacerbate a number of health issues.

People with bipolar illness may be especially vulnerable to the side effects of alcohol, even at modest consumption levels. The inability to sleep due to alcohol use might lead to emotional outbursts. Furthermore, alcohol can reduce the efficiency of medications, and excessive drinking can exacerbate several health issues, such as inflammation and liver damage.

Many diseases and conditions, including bipolar illness, include inflammation as a central contributor to their onset and course. For example, the oxidative stress caused by eating processed meals and drinking sugary beverages might lead to inflammation. Alterations in neurotransmitter levels in the brain are another mechanism through which inflammation can contribute to mood instability.

The importance of a healthy, balanced diet for those with bipolar illness cannot be overstated. Avoiding or limiting your intake of processed foods, sugary drinks, and alcohol is recommended because they have been linked to mood swings, inflammation, and weight gain. Supporting brain health and improving wellbeing may be accomplished by eating a diet high in whole, nutrient-dense foods including fruits, vegetables, lean protein, and healthy fats. It is crucial to collaborate with a healthcare provider to create a treatment plan that incorporates both medication and behavioral modifications.

5 30 Days Sample Meal Plan for a Bipolar Diet

BREAKFAST RECIPES FOR BIPOLAR DISORDER

Bread Bowl Quiche

Ingredients

for 8 servings

- 1 large loaf sourdough bread

- 10 slices cheddar cheese

- 18 large eggs

- 2 teaspoons salt

- 2 teaspoons pepper

- ½ lb bacon(225 g), cooked, chopped

- 1 cup shredded cheese blend(100 g)

- 1 cup broccoli(150 g), chopped, cooked

- 1 tablespoon fresh scallion, sliced

- 2 cups heavy cream(480 mL)

- 1 cup cherry tomatoes(200 g), halved

- mixed greens salad, for serving

Preparation

1. Preheat the oven to 350°F (180°C). Line baking sheet with aluminum foil and place a sheet of parchment paper over the foil.

2. With a serrated knife, cut off the top half-inch (1 cm) of the sourdough loaf. Cut around the edge of the bread, then use your fingers to remove the center and set aside for later.

3. Line the inside of the bread bowl with the sliced cheddar cheese.

4. Place the bread bowl on the baking sheet and wrap the outside with the parchment and foil.

5. Bake for 8 minutes, or until the cheese is melted.

6. In a large bowl, combine the eggs, salt, pepper, bacon, shredded cheese blend, broccoli, scallions, and heavy cream. Whisk until smooth, then add the cherry tomatoes.

7. Pour the egg mixture into the bread bowl, leaving a half-inch (1 cm) of space at the top. Cover the bread bowl with foil.

8. Bake for 1 hour and 40 minutes, or until the center of the quiche has set

9. Let cool for at least 30 minutes before slicing. Serve with a mixed green salad.

10. Enjoy!

Vegetarian Breakfast Apple Sausages

Ingredients

for 10 links

- 2 tablespoons olive oil, divided

- ½ cup onion(75 g), minced

- 2 cloves garlic, minced

- 1 cup apple(120 g), minced

- 1 cup baby bella mushroom(75 g), minced

- 1 teaspoon fennel seeds

- 1 teaspoon dried rosemary

- 1 teaspoon sage powder

- 1 tablespoon maple syrup

- salt, to taste

- pepper, to taste

- 15 oz cannellini bean(425 g), 1 can, drained and rinsed

- ½ cup chickpeas(100 g), canned, rinsed and drained, or cooked

- 1 cup vital wheat gluten(125 g), or all-purpose flour

Preparation

1. Heat 1 tablespoon of olive oil in a large skillet over medium heat. Add the onion and garlic and cook for about 4 minutes, until fragrant and the onion is translucent.

2. Add the apples, mushrooms, fennel seeds, rosemary, sage, maple syrup, salt, and pepper and stir to combine. Reduce the heat to medium-low and cook for about 10 minutes, until the mixture is tender and the liquid released from the mushrooms has evaporated. Remove from the heat and let cool.

3. Add the cannellini beans and chickpeas to a food processor and pulse into a smooth paste.

4. Transfer the bean paste to a large bowl and add the apple/mushroom mixture and vital wheat gluten. Mix with a spatula and then your hands until well combined.

5. Form the sausage mixture into a loaf, wrap in plastic wrap, and refrigerate for 2 hours.

6. Unwrap the chilled sausage mixture and divide into 10-12 equal pieces, depending on what size sausages you would like.

7. Roll a piece between your palms into a sausage shape. Place in the center of a large sheet of plastic wrap and roll the plastic over it so the sausage is completely encased. Twist the ends of the wrap and knot them together tightly. Repeat for each sausage.

8. Bring a large pot of water to a simmer. Plunge the wrapped sausages in the water and simmer for 45-50 minutes, until the sausages are firm.

9. Remove from the water and let cool for about 5 minutes, then unwrap.

10. Heat the remaining tablespoon of olive oil in a large skillet over medium-low heat. Fry the sausages for 1-2 minutes on each side, until golden brown.

11. Serve immediately or keep wrapped in the refrigerator for up to 4 days.

12. Enjoy!

Sweet Potato Breakfast Cups

Ingredients

for 12 breakfast cups

- 3 medium sweet potatoes, peeled

- 1 teaspoon salt, plus more to taste

- ½ teaspoon pepper, plus more to taste

- ½ teaspoon paprika

- 1 teaspoon garlic powder

- 1 teaspoon onion powder

- 2 tablespoons olive oil

- 1 cup shredded cheese blend (100 g)

FILLING SUGGESTIONS

EGG AND PEPPER

- 2 small eggs, beaten

- ¼ red bell pepper, seeded and diced

BROCCOLI, TOMATO, AND CHEESE

- ½ cup small broccoli floret (75 g)

- ½ cup cherry tomato (100 g), halved

- ¼ cup shredded cheese blend (25 g)

PEPPER, ONION, AND BACON

- ¼ red bell pepper, seeded and diced

- ¼ cup onion (40 g), diced

- 1 ½ strips bacon, cooked and diced

EGG AND BACON

- 3 small eggs

- 1 ½ strips bacon, cooked and diced

Preparation

1. Preheat the oven to 400°F (200°C).

2. With a mandolin or a sharp knife, carefully cut the sweet potatoes into 1/16-inch (1 mm) thick slices.

3. Place the sweet potato slices in a large bowl, add the salt, pepper, paprika, garlic powder, and onion powder, and toss the potatoes until evenly coated.

4. Let sit for about 20 minutes, until water releases from the sweet potatoes and the slices are soft and flexible.

5. Brush the cups of a 12-cup muffin tin with the olive oil.

6. Arrange 5 sweet potato slices around the sides of a muffin cup, overlapping slightly. Place 1 slice on the bottom to create a flower. Repeat with the remaining potato slices. Sprinkle a bit of cheese in the bottom of each cup.

7. Bake for 10 minutes until the cheese has melted and the sweet potato slices are tender.

8. Remove the potato cups from the oven and reduce the oven temperature to 300°F (150°C).

9. Add your desired fillings to the cups. Season with salt and pepper.

10. Bake for another 20-25 minutes, or until the eggs are completely cooked and/or the vegetables are tender. Let cool for about 5 minutes.

11. Serve warm.

12. Enjoy!

Thanksgiving Leftover Sweet Potato Waffles

Ingredients

for 5 waffles

WAFFLES

- 2 cups whole wheat(250 g)

- 1 tablespoon baking powder

- 1 teaspoon cinnamon

- ½ teaspoon salt

- 3 large eggs, room temperature

- 1 cup milk(240 mL)

- ¼ cup olive oil(60 mL)

- ¼ cup maple syrup(60 mL)

- 1 teaspoon vanilla extract

- 1 ½ cups mashed sweet potato(360 g)

- oil, of choice, for greasing

CRANBERRY SYRUP

- 1 cup cranberry sauce(275 g)

- ¼ cup orange juice(60 mL)

PECAN TOPPING

- 3 tablespoons maple syrup

- 1 pink lady apple

- ¼ cup water(60 mL)

- ½ cup raw pecans(75 g), roughly chopped

- 2 tablespoons crumbled goat cheese

Preparation

1. Make the waffles: In a medium bowl, whisk together the flour, baking powder, cinnamon, and salt.

2. In a separate large bowl, whisk together eggs, milk, olive oil, maple syrup, vanilla, and sweet potato until smooth.

3. Add the dry ingredients to the wet ingredients and stir with a rubber spatula until just combined, making sure not to overmix the batter.

4. Heat a waffle iron and grease with oil.

5. Scoop enough batter to fill your waffle iron into the center. Close the iron and cook for 5-6 minutes, until the waffle is golden brown and cooked all the way through. Remove the waffle and repeat with the remaining batter.

6. Make the cranberry syrup: Add the cranberry sauce and orange juice to a blender and blend until smooth. The syrup should be thin enough to drizzle, but not liquidy. Add more orange juice as needed to reach the right consistency. Set aside.

7. Make the pecan topping: In a small saucepan, combine the apple, pecans, maple syrup, and water. Cook over medium-high heat until the syrup starts to glaze the pecans and the apples soften, about 10 minutes.

8. Serve the waffles warm with the pecan topping, cranberry syrup, and a few pieces of goat cheese, if desired.

9. Enjoy!

Pineapple Carrot Cake Breakfast Bread

Ingredients

for 12 servings

BREAD

- oil, for greasing
- 1 ½ cups whole wheat flour (195 g)
- ⅓ cup organic sugar (65 g)
- 1 ½ teaspoons baking soda
- 1 ½ teaspoons baking powder
- 1 tablespoon ground cinnamon
- 1 teaspoon ground cardamom
- 2 teaspoons ground ginger
- ½ teaspoon ground cloves
- ½ teaspoon kosher salt

- ½ cup quick oat(40 g)

- 3 cups shredded carrots(330 g), about 3 large carrots

- 1 ½ cups crushed pineapple(565 g), 1 can, drained, juice reserved

- 3 large eggs, beaten

- ¼ cup butter(30 g), 1/2 stick, melted

- 1 cup walnuts(100 g), chopped, optional

GREEK YOGURT "FROSTING"

- 1 cup plain greek yogurt(245 g)

- 1 tablespoon maple syrup

Preparation

1. Preheat the oven to 375°F (190°C). Generously grease a 9 x 4 (22 x 10 cm) loaf pan with oil.

2. In a large bowl, sift together the flour, sugar, baking soda, baking powder, cinnamon, cardamom, ginger, cloves, and salt. Add the oats and whisk to combine.

3. In a separate large bowl, combine the shredded carrots, pineapple, eggs, and melted butter. Mix well.

4. Add the wet ingredients to the dry ingredients and stir until there are no dry clumps left. Gently fold in the walnuts, if using.

5. Pour the batter into the prepared loaf pan and smooth the top.

6. Bake for 1 hour, until a toothpick inserted in the center of the bread comes out clean.

7. While the bread is baking, make the Greek yogurt "frosting": In a small bowl, combine the Greek yogurt, maple syrup, and 2 tablespoons of the reserved pineapple juice. Stir until well incorporated. Chill in the refrigerator until ready to use.

8. Remove the bread from the oven and allow to cool for 10 minutes, until safe to handle. Remove from the loaf pan and let cool completely on a wire rack.

9. Slice the bread and serve with a smear of frosting.

10. Enjoy!

Easy Cast-Iron Cheesy Asparagus Quiche

Ingredients

for 8 servings

- olive oil, to taste
- 1 bunch asparagus, trimmed and chopped into 3-in (7 cm) pieces
- 2 teaspoons kosher salt, divided
- 2 teaspoons freshly ground black pepper, divided
- 8 tablespoons unsalted butter
- 2 cups all-purpose flour(250 g)
- ½ teaspoon baking powder
- ¾ cup grated parmesan cheese(80 g), divided
- ¼ cup cold water(60 mL)
- 6 large eggs
- ⅓ cup sour cream(75 g)

- ⅔ cup half-and-half (160 mL)

- 1 ½ cups shredded sharp cheddar cheese (150 g)

- 1 cup cherry tomatoes (200 g), halved

Preparation

1. Preheat the oven to 375°F (190°C).

2. Heat a drizzle of olive oil in a 10-inch (25 cm) cast-iron skillet over medium heat. Add the asparagus, ½ teaspoon salt, and ½ teaspoon pepper. Sauté for 5-6 minutes, until the asparagus is bright green but still firm. Turn off the heat. Transfer the asparagus to a bowl and set aside to cool.

3. Add the butter to the hot skillet and let it melt from the residual heat. Allow the pan to cool with the butter in it.

4. Once the cast iron is mostly cooled (warm to the touch is okay), add the flour, ½ teaspoon salt, 1 teaspoon black pepper, baking powder, and ½ cup Parmesan cheese, stirring with a spatula until the texture is sandy. Add the water and stir to combine. Using your hands, press the dough evenly over the bottom and about 2 inches (5 cm) up the sides of the pan. Use a fork to crimp the edges of the dough against the side of the pan. Set aside.

5. Add the eggs and sour cream to a medium bowl. Whisk to combine. Add the half-and-half, remaining teaspoon of salt, and remaining ½ teaspoon pepper and whisk until fully incorporated.

6. Scatter the cheddar cheese evenly over the crust. Arrange the asparagus over the cheese. Sprinkle the remaining ¼ cup (25 G) Parmesan evenly over the asparagus. Slowly pour the egg mixture into the skillet. Do not overfill. Top with the cherry tomatoes, cut sides up.

7. Carefully transfer the quiche to the oven and bake for 45-50 minutes, until the center is set and the edges are golden. Let cool for at least 30 minutes before serving.

8. Serve the quiche straight from the pan. Note: Use a spatula to cut, instead of a knife, so as not to scratch your pan.

9. Enjoy!

High-Protein Sweet And Savory Crepes

Ingredients

for 6 servings

SAVORY RATATOUILLE FILLING

- ½ cup yellow onion(75 g), thinly sliced

- ½ yellow bell pepper, seeded and diced into 1/4 in (6 mm) pieces

- ½ cup roma tomato(100 g), seeded and diced

- ½ cup zucchini(75 g), diced

- ¾ cup japanese eggplant(270 g), about 1 small - diced

- 2 cloves garlic, unpeeled

- 2 tablespoons olive oil

- 2 teaspoons fresh thyme, plus more for garnish

- ½ teaspoon kosher salt, plus more to taste

- ¼ teaspoon freshly ground black pepper, plus more to taste

- ¼ cup goat cheese(55 g), room temperature

SWEET CREPE FILLING

- 1 cup whole milk ricotta cheese(250 g)

- ½ cup strawberry(75 g), finely chopped, plus more for garnish, quartered

- ¼ cup blackberry(35 g), halved, plus more for garnish

- 1 teaspoon lemon zest

- 1 tablespoon honey, plus more for garnish

- whipped cream, for garnish

CREPES

- 6 large eggs

- 1 ½ cups unsweetened coconut milk(360 mL), full-fat canned

- ½ cup coconut flour(60 g)

- 1 tablespoon coconut oil, melted, plus more for greasing

- ½ teaspoon kosher salt

Preparation

1. If making the savory filling, preheat the oven to 450°F (230°C).

2. In a large bowl, toss together the onion, bell pepper, tomato, zucchini, eggplant, garlic, olive oil, thyme, salt, and pepper. Spread in an even layer on a large baking sheet.

3. Roast the vegetables until they are soft and caramelized, about 18 minutes, flipping halfway through. Set aside to cool.

4. When cool enough to handle, pick the garlic from the vegetables and remove the skin. Add to a large bowl and mash into a paste. Add the goat cheese and stir to combine, then add the vegetables and toss to coat. Season with salt and pepper.

5. Use immediately to fill the crepes, or store in an airtight container in the refrigerator for up to 3 days.

6. If making the sweet filling: In a small bowl, stir together the ricotta, strawberries, blackberries, lemon zest, and honey.

7. Use immediately to fill crepes, or store in an airtight container in the refrigerator up to 3 days.

8. Make the crepes: In a large bowl, combine the eggs, coconut milk, coconut flour, coconut oil, and salt.

9. Using an immersion blender, blend the ingredients to form a smooth batter, scraping down the sides of the bowl as needed.

10. Preheat a 9-inch (22 cm) nonstick skillet or crepe pan over medium heat. Add just enough oil to coat the pan, about ½ teaspoon. Swirl the pan to coat evenly.

11. Add ½ cup batter to the hot pan and swirl the pan around again until the batter evenly coats the bottom all the way to the edges. Cook for 4-5 minutes, or until the bottom of the crepe is golden brown in spots and the top is completely cooked through with no raw batter on the surface.

12. Add ¼ cup of your preferred filling to the top left quarter of the crepe. Using a small spatula or spoon, evenly spread the filling over that section, leaving a ½-inch (1 ¼ cm) border along the outside edge. Fold the bottom half of the crepe over the top half, then fold the right (unfilled) side over the left side to form a triangle. Use a rubber spatula to gently transfer the crepe to a plate. Repeat with the remaining batter and filling.

13. Garnish the savory crepes with more thyme and the sweet crepes with whipped cream, quartered strawberries, blackberries, and honey.

14. Enjoy!

Garden Vegetable Vegan Quiche

Ingredients

for 8 servings

CRUST

- ¾ cup all purpose flour(95 g), plus more for dusting

- ¾ cup whole wheat flour(95 g)

- ½ teaspoon kosher salt

- 8 tablespoons vegan butter, cubed and chilled

- ¼ cup cold water(60 mL), plus more a needed

FILLING

- 1 tablespoon olive oil

- 2 cups mushroom(150 g), thinly sliced

- 1 cup leek(90 g)

- 1 teaspoon kosher salt, divided

- 1 teaspoon black pepper, divided

- 1 cup cherry tomato(200 g)

- 4 cups fresh spinach(160 g)

- 1 package silken tofu

- 2 tablespoons nutritional yeast

- ½ teaspoon black salt, optional

- ½ teaspoon garlic powder

- ½ teaspoon paprika

- ¼ teaspoon ground turmeric

- ⅛ teaspoon cayenne pepper

SPECIAL EQUIPMENT

- dried chickpea, for baking

Preparation

1. Make the crust: In a large bowl, mix together the all-purpose flour, whole-wheat flour, and salt. Add the butter and, using your hands, work it into the flour until only pea-sized pieces remain. Continue working with your hands until the dough has a shaggy texture.

2. Add the water, starting with 3 tablespoons, and mix until the dough is moist enough to hold together. Add more water as needed, 1 tablespoon at a time. Form the dough into a disc and wrap in plastic wrap. Refrigerate for 30-60 minutes.

3. Preheat the oven to 350°F (180°C).

4. Make the filling: Heat the olive oil in a large skillet over medium-high heat. Once the oil is shimmering, add the mushrooms. Sauté for 3-5 minutes, until the mushrooms are beginning to brown lightly. Reduce the heat to medium and add the leeks, ½ teaspoon kosher salt, and ½ teaspoon pepper. Cook for another 3-5 minutes, until the leeks have softened slightly. Add the tomatoes

and cook for 1 minute, until slightly softened. Add the spinach and sauté for 1-2 minutes, until just wilted. Remove the pan from the heat.

5. Lightly dust a clean surface with flour. Roll out the dough, turning it frequently so it doesn't stick, to a 12-inch (30 cm) round, about ⅛-inch (3 mm) thick.

6. Gently transfer the crust to a 9-inch (22 cm) pie dish. Trim any excess dough around the edges. Fold the edges of dough back underneath itself, then crimp using an index finger knuckle on one hand and the thumb and index finger on the other hand.

7. Crumple a piece of parchment paper, then spread it out in the center of the crust. Add the dried beans to the center and spread toward the sides of the crust--this will add weight to keep the crust from puffing up and hold up the walls while baking.

8. Bake the crust for 15 minutes. Carefully remove the weights by lifting out the parchment paper, then bake for 5 minutes more, until the dough no longer looks raw.

9. Carefully pour the silken tofu into a fine-mesh strainer set over a bowl. Let sit for 10 minutes to allow the excess water to drain.

10. Add the tofu, nutritional yeast, remaining ½ teaspoon salt, remaining ½ teaspoon pepper, black salt, garlic powder, paprika, turmeric, and cayenne to a blender. Puree until smooth.

11. Spread half the sautéed vegetables evenly over the bottom of the crust. Pour the tofu puree over the vegetables, then add the remaining vegetables on top..

12. Bake for 40-45 minutes, until the center no longer jiggles and the crust is just beginning to brown.

13. Let the quiche cool for at least 30 minutes before slicing to allow the filling to set.

14. Enjoy!

Eggs In Purgatory

Ingredients

for 2 servings

- 2 tablespoons olive oil

- ½ medium yellow onion, diced

- ⅓ cup water(80 mL)

- 10 oz cherry tomatoes(285 g)

- kosher salt, to taste

- freshly ground black pepper, to taste

- 2 large eggs

Preparation

1. Heat the olive oil in a small skillet over medium heat. Add the onion and cook until softened, about 5 minutes.

2. Add the water and tomatoes and season with salt and pepper. Cover and cook until the tomatoes start to burst but still hold some of their shape, 5–7 minutes.

3. Using the back of a spoon, create 2 wells in the tomato mixture. Crack an egg into each well. Season with salt and pepper.

4. Cook uncovered for 5–6 minutes, until the egg whites are set but the yolks are still a bit runny.

5. Serve immediately.

6. Enjoy!

Steak And Eggs Hash

Ingredients

for 4 servings

- 2 lb yukon gold potato(910 g), peeled and cut into 1/2 in (1 1/2 cm)

- cold water, for cooking potatoes

- 1 ½ tablespoons kosher salt, divided

- 1 top sirloin steak

- 1 ½ teaspoons freshly ground black pepper, divided

- 2 tablespoons unsalted butter, divided

- 1 tablespoon canola oil

- ½ small yellow onion, thinly sliced

- 8 oz cremini mushroom(225 g), steemed and quartered

- 1 small red bell pepper, seeded and diced

- 1 teaspoon fresh oregano, chopped

- 1 cup cherry tomato(200 g), halved

- 4 large eggs

- 1 tablespoon fresh parsley, minced

Preparation

1. Add the potatoes to a large pot and fill with enough cold water to cover by 1 inch (2 ½ cm). Season with 1½ teaspoons of salt and bring to a boil over medium-high heat. Boil for 5 minutes, then drain and run under cold water to stop the potatoes from cooking further. Dry the potatoes with paper towels and set aside.

2. Place a rack in the lower third of the oven. Preheat the oven to 350°F (180°C)

3. Blot the steak dry with a paper towel and season on both sides with 1½ teaspoons of salt and 1 teaspoon black pepper.

4. Heat a 10-inch (25 cm) cast iron skillet over high heat until smoking. Reduce the heat to medium-high. Add 1 tablespoon of butter and the canola oil to the pan and melt the butter completely, about 1 minute. Add the seasoned steak and cook, without disturbing, for 2 minutes on each side. The steak will be rare, but will finish cooking in the oven. Transfer to a cutting board to rest for at least 5 minutes before slicing into ¼-inch (6 mm) strips.

5. Reduce the heat to medium and melt the remaining tablespoon of butter in the same skillet. Add the onion, mushrooms, red bell pepper, and ½ teaspoon of salt. Cook, stirring occasionally, until the onions are slightly caramelized and the mushrooms have released their liquid, 8–10 minutes.

6. Add the potatoes to the skillet and season with the remaining teaspoon of salt, ¼ teaspoon black pepper, and the oregano. Stir to combine and cook, without disturbing, for 4 minutes, until the potatoes are golden brown and crisp on one side. Add the cherry tomatoes and stir to combine.

7. Make 4 wells in the hash using the back of a spoon and carefully crack an egg into each well.

8. Scatter the sliced steak on top of the hash and transfer to the oven. Bake for 10 minutes, or until the egg whites are set but the yolks are still runny.

9. Remove the hash from the oven and season with the remaining ¼ teaspoon pepper. Garnish with the parsley.

10. Serve warm.

11. Enjoy!

Stocked Brooklyn's Sweet Potato "Toast"

Ingredients

for 4 servings

- 2 medium sweet potatoes

- 3 tablespoons avocado oil

- ½ teaspoon pepper, optional

- 3 tablespoons olive oil

- 1 cup dry quinoa (175 g)

- 1 teaspoon coconut amino

- 8 oz fresh goat cheese (225 g), (equal to one small log)

- 2 tablespoons milk

- 1 teaspoon apple cider vinegar

- ⅛ teaspoon sweet paprika, optional

- 2 sprigs fresh tarragon, or herb of choice

- 8 kale chips, optional

- 4 eggs, optional

Preparation

1. PREPARE THE POTATOES:

2. Preheat the oven to 375°F. Line a sheet tray with parchment paper.

3. Wash and cut the potatoes lengthwise into ¾-inch slices. Rub with 2 tablespoons of avocado oil. Dust with pepper and a pinch of salt.

4. Evenly space the toasts on the sheet tray. Roast until lightly browned, about 15 minutes. Remove from the oven and let cool.

5. PREPARE THE QUINOA:

6. Rinse the quinoa in a fine-mesh strainer.

7. Add 2 tablespoons of olive oil to a pot with a tight-fitting lid set on medium heat. When the oil is shimmering, add the quinoa. Stir to coat, then cook until fragrant and lightly toasted, about 2 minutes.

8. Add 2 cups (480 ml) of water and a pinch of salt to the pot, then increase the heat and cover. As soon as the liquid comes to a boil, turn down the heat to create a gentle simmer.

9. Cook until the water is absorbed, about 20 minutes. Remove from the heat, uncover, and add the coconut aminos, using a fork to fluff and stir the quinoa.

10. Heat the remaining avocado oil in a skillet set on medium heat. When the oil is shimmering, add half the quinoa and stir to coat. Cook, stirring occasionally, until golden brown and crispy, about 15 minutes. Transfer to a plate lined with a paper towel. Then, repeat the process with the remaining quinoa.

11. PREPARE THE CHEESE:

12. Add the goat cheese, milk, and apple cider vinegar to a small food processor. To this, add the paprika.

13. Wash and chop the herbs, including any delicate stems, then add to the food processor. Blend until smooth.

14. TO SERVE:

15. Heat the "toasts" and place one or two slices on each plate.

16. Crumble a spoonful or two of the cheese spread on top of each serving.

17. Fry one egg per person and place it on top of each serving of toast. Crumble more cheese spread on top of the fried eggs.

18. Sprinkle each serving generously with the crispy quinoa.

19. Crush the kale chips and sprinkle on top of each serving.

20. Plate and serve.

Almond Butter Cucumber Crunch Sandwich

Ingredients

for 2 servings

- 4 slices whole wheat bread, lightly toasted

- 4 tablespoons Justin's® Classic Almond Butter

- 1 green apple, thinly sliced

- 2 persian cucumbers, thinly sliced

- 1 avocado, thinly sliced

- 1 teaspoon hemp hearts

Preparation

1. Spread the Justin's® Almond Butter evenly over each slice of bread.

2. Layer the apple, cucumber, and avocado slices on 2 slices of bread. Sprinkle the hemp hearts evenly on top.

3. Top each piece with the remaining slice of bread, almond butter side down. Gently slice in half on the diagonal.

4. Enjoy!

Southwestern One-pan Shakshuka

Ingredients

for 1 serving

- 2 teaspoons olive oil

- 1 clove garlic, minced

- 1 small red onion, diced

- ½ teaspoon salt

- ¼ teaspoon ground black pepper

- ¼ teaspoon red pepper flakes

- 1 ½ cups crushed tomato(300 g)

- 2 large eggs

- ¼ avocado, diced

- ¼ cup cherry tomato(50 g), halved

- 2 tablespoons fresh cilantro, chopped

Preparation

1. Preheat oven to 350 °F (180 °C).

2. Heat olive oil in an oven-safe skillet over medium heat.

3. Once the oil is shimmering, add the garlic, ½ of the onion red onion, salt, pepper, and red pepper flakes, and cook until the onion is softened, about 3 minutes.

4. Add the crushed tomatoes and stir, bringing the mixture to a simmer.

5. Crack the eggs directly into the tomato mixture, and transfer to the oven.

6. Bake until eggs are set, about 11 minutes.

7. Top with avocado, cherry tomatoes, cilantro, and remaining red onion.

8. Enjoy!

Egg, Avocado, & Tomato Toast

Ingredients

for 1 serving

- 1 slice bread

- 1 avocado

- 2 cherry tomatoes, sliced

- 1 egg

Preparation

1. Sliced two cherry tomatoes.

2. Mash ½ of 1 avocado with salt. (Use the other half for another toast.)

3. Prepare bread in a toaster to desired crispiness.

4. In a pan, fry an egg sunny side up.

5. Assemble the toast by spreading avocado on the toast, then the tomatoes and topping everything with the egg.

6. Enjoy!

Pear & Honey Sweet Potato Toast

Ingredients

for 1 serving

- 1 sweet potato

- ricotta cheese, to taste

- 2 slices pear

- honey, to taste

Preparation

1. Cut sweet potato into thin slices, about ¼ inch (6 mm) thick.

2. Place in toaster and set it to the maximum cook time. When it pops, flip the sweet potato slices over and toast 1 more time. Depending on the strength

of your toaster and your preferences, you may need to toast it 1 more time after that.

3. Remove from toaster and let cool enough to handle.

4. Spread ricotta evenly across sweet potato toast.

5. Slice pear thinly and place on top of ricotta. Drizzle with honey.

6. Enjoy!

Chickpea Flour Omelet

Ingredients

for 2 servings

FILLING

- olive oil, for cooking

- ½ cup cremini mushroom(35 g), sliced

- ½ cup cherry tomatoes(100 g), halved

- salt, to taste

- pepper, to taste

- 1 clove garlic, minced

- 2 cups fresh spinach(80 g)

OMELET

- ¾ cup chickpea flour(90 g)

- 1 ½ tablespoons nutritional yeast

- ½ teaspoon baking soda

- ½ teaspoon garlic powder

- ¼ teaspoon turmeric

- ¼ teaspoon salt

- ⅛ teaspoon pepper

- ⅛ teaspoon black salt, kala namak, optional

- 1 teaspoon apple cider vinegar

- ¾ cup unsweetened almond milk(180 mL)

- fresh cilantro, for serving

- salsa, for serving

Preparation

1. In a medium nonstick saucepan, heat a drizzle of olive oil over medium heat. Once the oil begins to shimmer, add the mushrooms and tomatoes and cook for 3-4 minutes, until they start to release their juices. Season with salt and pepper.

2. Add a bit more olive oil to the pan, then add the garlic and cook for 2 minutes, until fragrant.

3. Add the spinach and cook for 3-4 minutes, until wilted. Remove the pan from the heat.

4. In a medium bowl, combine the chickpea flour, nutritional yeast, baking soda, garlic powder, turmeric, salt, black salt, apple cider vinegar, and almond milk, and whisk together until mostly smooth.

5. In a medium nonstick saucepan, heat a drizzle of olive oil over medium heat. Once the oil begins to shimmer, add a ½ cup (120 ml) of the omelet batter to the pan. Let cook for 5-7 minutes, or until several bubbles have formed on the surface. Spoon half of the vegetable filling onto one side of the omelet.

6. Using a spatula, fold the omelet in half. Turn off the heat and cover the pan with a lid. Let the omelet steam for 5 minutes, until completely cooked through. Repeat with the remaining omelet batter and filling.

7. Serve the omelets with salsa and fresh cilantro.

8. Enjoy!

Protein-Packed Breakfast Bars

Ingredients

for 24 bars

BASE

- ¼ cup flax meal(40 g)

- ¾ cup water(180 mL)

- 6 cups rolled oats(540 g)

- 6 cups quinoa(1 kg), cooked

- 4 teaspoons baking powder

- 1 teaspoon salt

- 1 cup maple syrup (220 g)

- ½ cup refined coconut oil (120 mL), melted

- 2 teaspoons vanilla extract

- 4 ripe bananas, mashed

FILLINGS

PEANUT BUTTER CHOCOLATE CHIP

- 6 tablespoons peanut butter

- 5 tablespoons mini chocolate chips

APPLE CINNAMON

- ¾ cup gala apple (90 g), diced

- 6 tablespoons walnuts, chopped

- 1 ½ tablespoons cinnamon

- ¼ teaspoon nutmeg

CARROT CAKE

- ¾ cup carrot(30 g), grated

- 3 teaspoons cinnamon

- ¼ teaspoon nutmeg

- 3 tablespoons almond butter

MIXED BERRY

- 3 tablespoons almond butter

- ⅓ cup Strawberries(55 g), diced

- ⅓ cup raspberries(40 g)

- ⅓ cup blueberries(40 g)

- nonstick cooking spray

Preparation

1. Preheat the oven to 375°F (190°C).

2. To make the flax eggs, combine the flax meal and water in a small bowl and mix well. Set aside for 10 minutes to gel.

3. In a large bowl, combine the oats, quinoa, baking powder, salt, maple syrup, coconut oil, vanilla, flax eggs, and bananas, and mix until well-combined.

4. Divide the base dough equally between 4 medium bowls.

5. Add the peanut butter and chocolate chips to 1 bowl and mix until combined.

6. Add the apple, walnuts, cinnamon, and nutmeg to another bowl and mix until combined.

7. Add the carrots, cinnamon, nutmeg, and almond butter to another bowl and mix until combined.

8. Add the almond butter, strawberries, raspberries, and blueberries to the last bowl and mix until combined.

9. Grease 2 9x13-inch (23x33-cm) baking pans with nonstick spray. Transfer the bar mixtures to the pans, packing each mixture into half of a pan with a spoon or spatula.

10. Bake for 25-30 minutes, until the edges are slightly golden brown.

11. Remove the pans from the oven and let the bars cool for 20 minutes, then refrigerate for at least 30 minutes, or up to 5 days. Gently cut each flavor into 6 bars, then remove from the pans with a spatula.

12. Enjoy!

Simple Shakshuka

Ingredients

for 4 servings

- olive oil, drizzle

- 1 cup yellow onion(150 g), diced

- 1 orange bell pepper, diced

- salt, to taste

- pepper, to taste

- ½ teaspoon cumin

- ½ teaspoon paprika

- 3 cloves garlic, chopped

- 28 oz crushed tomatoes(795 g), 1 can

- 1 bay leaf

- 1 ½ cups fresh baby kale(100 g)

- 4 large eggs

- ¼ cup feta cheese(25 g), crumble

- bread, toasted, for serving

Preparation

1. Heat a large cast iron skillet over medium-low heat.

2. Once the pan is hot, add the olive oil and swirl to coat the pan. Add the onion, bell pepper, salt, and pepper. Sauté 5 minutes, or until the onion is almost translucent.

3. Add the cumin, paprika, and garlic. Sauté 2-3 minutes, or until the garlic is slightly brown.

4. Pour in the crushed tomatoes and add the bay leaf. Simmer for 10-15 minutes, or until the mixture has thickened.

5. Stir in the baby kale until wilted.

6. Reduce the heat to low, then carefully crack the eggs into the sauce. Cover and simmer until the egg whites are set, about 10-12 minutes.

7. Top with the feta cheese and remove the pan from the heat.

8. Enjoy!

Breakfast Taco Cups

Ingredients

for 12 cups

- nonstick cooking spray, for greasing

- 3 large flour tortillas

- ¾ cup vegetarian refried beans(180 g)

- ¾ cup egg(165 g), scrambled

- ¼ cup shredded mexican cheese blend(25 g)

- 3 cherry tomatoes, quartered

- fresh cilantro leaf, for garnish

Preparation

1. Preheat the oven to 375°F (190°C). Generously coat a 12-cup muffin tin with nonstick spray.

2. Stack the tortillas and cut off the edges so the tortillas are square. Then, quarter the squares so you have 12 small tortilla pieces.

3. Press a tortilla square into each cup of the prepared muffin tin.

4. Fill each cup with 1 tablespoon of refried beans, 1 tablespoon of scrambled eggs, and 1 teaspoon of cheese and top with a cherry tomato quarter.

5. Bake for about 10 minutes, until the edges of the tortillas are golden brown and the cheese has melted.

6. Garnish with cilantro.

7. Enjoy!

Broccoli Cheddar Brunch Bake

Ingredients

for 4 servings

- 12 eggs, whisked

- salt, to taste

- pepper, to taste

- ½ onion, diced

- ½ cup shredded cheddar cheese(50 g)

- 1 cup cherry tomato(200 g), halved

- 1 head small broccoli floret

- scallion, for garnish, optional

Preparation

1. Preheat oven to 325°F (160°C).

2. In a large bowl, whisk 12 eggs with salt and pepper.

3. Add onion and cheese and combine.

4. In an oiled baking dish, add tomatoes, broccoli, and egg mixture.

5. Bake for 30-45 minutes or until golden and eggs are set.

6. Garnish with scallions.

7. Enjoy!

LUNCH RECIPES FOR BIPOLAR DISORDER

Mixed Green Salad with Grilled Chicken

Ingredients

- Mixed salad greens (spinach, arugula, lettuce)

- Grilled chicken breast (sliced)

- Cherry tomatoes (halved)

- Cucumber (sliced)

- Red onion (thinly sliced)

- Avocado (sliced)

- Fresh berries (strawberries, blueberries, raspberries)

- Balsamic vinaigrette (or dressing of your choice)

Instructions

1. In a large bowl, combine the mixed salad greens, cherry tomatoes, cucumber, red onion, and avocado.

2. Add the grilled chicken slices on top.

3. Sprinkle fresh berries over the salad.

4. Drizzle with balsamic vinaigrette or your preferred dressing.

5. Toss gently to combine and enjoy a refreshing and filling salad.

Veggie Wrap

Instructions

- Whole-grain tortilla or wrap

- Hummus

- Spinach leaves

- Shredded carrots

- Sliced bell peppers (red, yellow, or green)

- Sliced cucumber

- Sliced avocado

- Sprouts (such as alfalfa sprouts)

Salt and pepper to taste

Instructions

1. Lay the tortilla flat and spread a generous amount of hummus on it.

2. Layer spinach leaves, shredded carrots, bell peppers, cucumber, avocado, and sprouts on top.

3. Season with salt and pepper.

4. Roll up the tortilla tightly, tucking in the sides as you go.

5. Slice the wrap in half or into smaller portions for easy handling.

6. Serve with a side of fresh fruit or a light yogurt dip.

Quinoa and Roasted Vegetable Bowl:

Instructions

- Cooked quinoa

- Mixed roasted vegetables (such as bell peppers, zucchini, eggplant, and cherry tomatoes)

- Fresh herbs (such as basil or cilantro)

- Lemon juice

- Olive oil

- Salt and pepper to taste

Instructions:

1. Preheat the oven to 400°F (200°C).

2. Toss the mixed vegetables with olive oil, salt, and pepper. Spread them on a baking sheet and roast for 20-25 minutes until tender and slightly caramelized.

3. In a bowl, combine the cooked quinoa with the roasted vegetables.

4. Squeeze fresh lemon juice over the mixture and add fresh herbs.

5. Toss gently to combine all the ingredients.

6. Adjust seasoning if needed.

7. Serve warm as a flavorful and nutritious lunch option.

Fruit and Spinach Salad:

Instructions

- Spinach leaves

- Fresh strawberries (sliced)

- Mandarin orange segments

- Sliced almonds

- Goat cheese crumbles (optional)

- Balsamic vinaigrette or citrus dressing

Instructions

1. In a large bowl, combine the spinach leaves, sliced strawberries, mandarin orange segments, sliced almonds, and goat cheese crumbles (if using).

2. Drizzle with your choice of balsamic vinaigrette or citrus dressing.

3. Toss gently to combine all the ingredients.

4. Serve as a refreshing and nutritious salad option.

Grilled Vegetable Panini:

Instructions

- Whole-grain bread

- Grilled or roasted vegetables (such as zucchini, eggplant, bell peppers, and red onions)

- Fresh basil leaves

- Sliced mozzarella cheese

- Pesto sauce

Instructions

1. Spread pesto sauce on one side of each slice of bread.

2. Layer grilled or roasted vegetables, fresh basil leaves, and sliced mozzarella cheese on one slice of bread.

3. Top with the other slice of bread, pesto side down.

4. Heat a panini press or grill pan over medium heat.

5. Place the sandwich in the panini press or grill pan and cook until the bread is toasted and the cheese is melted.

6. Remove from heat, slice the panini in half, and serve with a side of fresh fruit.

Chickpea and Vegetable Stir-Fry:

Instructions

- Cooked chickpeas

- Assorted stir-fry vegetables (such as broccoli, bell peppers, snap peas, carrots, and mushrooms)

- Garlic cloves (minced)

- Ginger (grated)

- Low-sodium soy sauce (or tamari for a gluten-free option)

- Sesame oil

- Lime juice

- Sesame seeds (for garnish)

Instructions

1. Heat sesame oil in a large pan or wok over medium heat.

2. Add minced garlic and grated ginger, and sauté for a minute until fragrant.

3. Add the stir-fry vegetables and cooked chickpeas to the pan, and stir-fry for a few minutes until the vegetables are tender-crisp.

4. Drizzle soy sauce and lime juice over the stir-fry and toss to coat evenly.

5. Cook for another minute, then remove from heat.

6. Garnish with sesame seeds and serve over a bed of cooked quinoa or brown rice, or enjoy it as is.

Caprese Salad Sandwich:

Instructions

- Whole-grain bread
- Fresh mozzarella cheese slices
- Tomato slices
- Fresh basil leaves
- Balsamic glaze
- Salt and pepper to taste

Instructions

1. Take two slices of whole-grain bread.

2. Layer fresh mozzarella cheese slices, tomato slices, and fresh basil leaves on one slice of bread.

3. Drizzle balsamic glaze over the ingredients and sprinkle with salt and pepper.

4. Top with the other slice of bread.

5. Cut the sandwich in half or into smaller portions.

6. Enjoy a delicious and simple caprese salad sandwich.

Rainbow Veggie Sushi Rolls:

Instructions

- Sushi Nori sheets

- Cooked sushi rice

- Assorted thinly sliced vegetables (such as cucumber, bell peppers, carrots, avocado, and radishes)

- Soy sauce or tamari (for dipping)

Instructions

1. Place a sushi mat on a clean surface.

2. Lay a sheet of sushi nori on top of the sushi mat.

3. Spread a thin layer of sushi rice evenly over the nori, leaving a small border at the top.

4. Arrange the sliced vegetables in colorful rows across the rice.

5. Using the sushi mat, roll the nori tightly, applying gentle pressure to secure the ingredients.

6. Wet the border of the nori with a little water to seal the roll.

7. Repeat the process with the remaining nori sheets and ingredients.

8. Once all the rolls are prepared, slice them into bite-sized pieces using a sharp knife.

9. Serve with soy sauce or tamari for dipping.

Fruit and Yogurt Parfait

Instructions

- Greek yogurt

- Mixed fresh fruits (such as berries, sliced bananas, and diced mango)

- Granola or crushed nuts

- Honey or maple syrup (optional)

Instructions

1. In a glass or jar, start layering with a spoonful of Greek yogurt at the bottom.

2. Add a layer of mixed fresh fruits on top of the yogurt.

3. Sprinkle a layer of granola or crushed nuts.

4. Repeat the layers until the glass or jar is filled, ending with a fruit layer on top.

5. Drizzle honey or maple syrup on top if desired.

6. Refrigerate for a few minutes to allow the flavors to meld together.

7. Enjoy a refreshing and satisfying fruit and yogurt parfait.

Roasted Vegetable and Quinoa Salad:

Instructions

- Cooked quinoa

- Assorted roasted vegetables (such as sweet potatoes, Brussels sprouts, cauliflower, and beets)

- Baby spinach or mixed greens

- Toasted walnuts or almonds

- Dried cranberries or raisins

- Lemon vinaigrette dressing

Instructions

1. In a large bowl, combine cooked quinoa, roasted vegetables, baby spinach or mixed greens, toasted walnuts or almonds, and dried cranberries or raisins.

2. Drizzle with lemon vinaigrette dressing and toss gently to combine.

3. Adjust seasoning if needed.

4. Serve as a hearty and nutritious salad.

Veggie and Hummus Wrap:

Instructions

- Whole-grain tortilla or wrap

- Hummus

- Sliced cucumber

- Shredded carrots

- Sliced bell peppers (red, yellow, or green)

- Sliced avocado

- Baby spinach or lettuce leaves

- Salt and pepper to taste

Instructions

1. Spread a generous amount of hummus on a whole-grain tortilla or wrap.

2. Layer sliced cucumber, shredded carrots, bell peppers, sliced avocado, and baby spinach or lettuce leaves on top of the hummus.

3. Season with salt and pepper.

4. Roll up the tortilla tightly, tucking in the sides as you go.

5. Slice the wrap in half or into smaller portions for easy handling.

6. Serve with a side of fresh fruit or vegetable sticks.

Fresh Fruit Salad with Yogurt

Instructions

- Assorted fresh fruits (such as watermelon, cantaloupe, pineapple, grapes, and kiwi)

- Greek yogurt

- Honey or maple syrup (optional)

- Chopped mint leaves (optional)

Instructions

1. Cut the fresh fruits into bite-sized pieces and place them in a large bowl.

2. In a separate bowl, mix Greek yogurt with honey or maple syrup if desired.

3. Pour the yogurt mixture over the fresh fruits and gently toss to coat.

4. Sprinkle chopped mint leaves on top for added freshness (optional).

5. Serve as a light and refreshing fruit salad.

Sweet Potato and Black Bean Burrito Bowl:

Instructions

• Cooked brown rice

• Roasted sweet potatoes (cubed)

• Black beans (canned or cooked)

• Sliced avocado

• Sliced cherry tomatoes

• Chopped red onion

• Fresh cilantro (chopped)

• Lime juice

- Chipotle or salsa dressing

Instructions

1. In a bowl, layer cooked brown rice, roasted sweet potatoes, black beans, sliced avocado, cherry tomatoes, and chopped red onion.

2. Drizzle with lime juice and chipotle or salsa dressing.

3. Sprinkle fresh cilantro on top.

4. Toss gently to combine all the ingredients.

5. Enjoy a flavorful and filling burrito bowl.

Zucchini Noodles with Pesto and Cherry Tomatoes:

Instructions

- Zucchini (spiralized into noodles)

- Homemade or store-bought pesto sauce

- Cherry tomatoes (halved)

- Pine nuts (toasted)

- Grated Parmesan cheese (optional)

- Fresh basil leaves (for garnish)

Instructions

1. In a pan, sauté the zucchini noodles for a few minutes until slightly softened.

2. Transfer the zucchini noodles to a serving plate.

3. Toss the zucchini noodles with pesto sauce until well coated.

4. Top with halved cherry tomatoes, toasted pine nuts, and grated Parmesan cheese (if using).

5. Garnish with fresh basil leaves.

6. Serve as a light and flavorful lunch option.

Spinach and Berry Smoothie Bowl:

Instructions

- Frozen mixed berries (such as strawberries, blueberries, and raspberries)

- Fresh spinach leaves

- Greek yogurt

- Almond milk (or any preferred milk)

- Toppings: sliced bananas, granola, chia seeds, shredded coconut, and fresh berries

Instructions

1. In a blender, combine frozen mixed berries, fresh spinach leaves, Greek yogurt, and almond milk.

2. Blend until smooth and creamy.

3. Pour the smoothie into a bowl.

4. Top with sliced bananas, granola, chia seeds, shredded coconut, and fresh berries.

5. Enjoy a refreshing and nutritious smoothie bowl.

Mediterranean Chickpea Salad

Instructions

- Canned chickpeas (drained and rinsed)

- Cucumber (diced)

- Cherry tomatoes (halved)

- Kalamata olives (pitted and halved)

- Red onion (thinly sliced)

- Fresh parsley (chopped)

- Feta cheese (crumbled)

- Lemon juice

- Extra virgin olive oil

- Salt and pepper to taste

Instructions

1. In a large bowl, combine chickpeas, diced cucumber, cherry tomatoes, Kalamata olives, red onion, chopped parsley, and crumbled feta cheese.

2. Drizzle with lemon juice and extra virgin olive oil.

3. Season with salt and pepper to taste.

4. Toss gently to combine all the ingredients.

5. Serve as a refreshing and protein-packed salad.

Veggie Quesadillas

Instructions

- Whole wheat tortillas

- Assorted sliced vegetables (such as bell peppers, zucchini, mushrooms, and onions)

- Shredded cheese (such as cheddar or Monterey Jack)

- Salsa or guacamole (for serving)

Instructions

1. Heat a non-stick skillet or griddle over medium heat.

2. Place a tortilla on the skillet and layer one side with sliced vegetables and shredded cheese.

3. Fold the tortilla in half, pressing down gently.

4. Cook for a few minutes on each side until the tortilla is crisp and the cheese is melted.

5. Remove from the skillet and cut into wedges.

6. Repeat with the remaining tortillas and filling.

7. Serve the quesadillas with salsa or guacamole for dipping.

Rainbow Fruit Skewers with Yogurt Dip:

Instructions

- Assorted fresh fruits (such as strawberries, pineapple, grapes, kiwi, and melon)

- Wooden skewers

- Greek yogurt

- Honey or maple syrup

- Vanilla extract

Instructions

1. Cut the fresh fruits into bite-sized pieces.

2. Thread the fruits onto wooden skewers, alternating colors to create a rainbow effect.

3. In a small bowl, mix Greek yogurt with honey or maple syrup and a splash of vanilla extract.

4. Serve the fruit skewers with the yogurt dip on the side.

5. Enjoy a fun and nutritious fruit snack or dessert.

Quinoa and Roasted Vegetable Stuffed Bell Peppers:

Instructions

- Bell peppers (any color)

- Cooked quinoa

- Roasted vegetables (such as broccoli, cauliflower, carrots, and onions)

- Goat cheese (crumbled)

- Fresh parsley (chopped)

- Olive oil

- Salt and pepper to taste

Instructions

1. Preheat the oven to 375°F (190°C).

2. Cut off the tops of the bell peppers and remove the seeds and membranes.

3. In a large bowl, combine cooked quinoa, roasted vegetables, crumbled goat cheese, chopped parsley, olive oil, salt, and pepper.

4. Stuff the bell peppers with the quinoa and roasted vegetable mixture.

5. Place the stuffed peppers in a baking dish and cover with foil.

6. Bake for 25-30 minutes until the peppers are tender and the filling is heated through.

7. Serve as a flavorful and satisfying stuffed bell pepper dish.

Greek Salad with Grilled Chicken

Instructions

- Grilled chicken breast (sliced)

- Mixed salad greens

- Cherry tomatoes (halved)

- Cucumber (sliced)

- Kalamata olives (pitted)

- Red onion (thinly sliced)

- Feta cheese (crumbled)

- Fresh oregano leaves

- Lemon juice

- Extra virgin olive oil

- Salt and pepper to taste

Instructions

1. In a large salad bowl, combine mixed salad greens, cherry tomatoes, cucumber slices, Kalamata olives, red onion slices, and crumbled feta cheese.

2. Add the grilled chicken breast slices on top.

3. Drizzle with lemon juice and extra virgin olive oil.

4. Season with salt and pepper to taste.

5. Garnish with fresh oregano leaves.

6. Toss gently to coat all the ingredients.

7. Enjoy a light and protein-packed Greek salad.

Veggie and Quinoa Stuffed Portobello Mushrooms

Instructions

- Portobello mushrooms (stems removed)

- Cooked quinoa

- Assorted sautéed vegetables (such as spinach, bell peppers, onions, and garlic)

- Crumbled goat cheese

- Fresh basil leaves (chopped)

- Balsamic glaze (for drizzling)

- Olive oil

- Salt and pepper to taste

Instructions

1. Preheat the oven to 375°F (190°C).

2. Place the portobello mushrooms on a baking sheet and brush them with olive oil.

3. Season with salt and pepper.

4. In a bowl, combine cooked quinoa, sautéed vegetables, crumbled goat cheese, and chopped basil leaves.

5. Fill each portobello mushroom cap with the quinoa and vegetable mixture.

6. Bake in the preheated oven for 15-20 minutes until the mushrooms are tender and the filling is heated through.

7. Drizzle with balsamic glaze before serving.

8. Enjoy a flavorful and satisfying stuffed mushroom dish.

DINNER RECIPES FOR BIPOLAR DISORDER

Naco Taco

Ingredients

for 4 Nacos

- 4 10-inch flour tortillas

- 2 tablespoons canola oil

- 1 onion medium yellow onion, diced

- 4 cloves garlic cloves, minced

- 1 lb ground beef

- 1 tablespoon ancho chile powder

- 1 tablespoon ground cumin

- 1 teaspoon ground coriander

- 2 teaspoons smoked paprika

- 1 teaspoon ground black pepper

- 1 teaspoon cornstarch

- 1 teaspoon kosher salt

- 1 tablespoon orange zest

- 1 block 16-ounce block processed American cheese, such as Velveeta

- 1 can 10-ounce can of diced tomatoes with chiles, such as Ro-tel

- ⅓ cup water

- 1 cup tortilla chips

- 1 cup shredded lettuce

- 1 cup guacamole

- ½ cup roma tomato, diced

- ½ cup sliced pickled jalapeños

- ¼ cup sour cream

Preparation

1. Preheat the oven to 350°F (180°C).

2. Make the tortilla shells: Cut each tortilla into a 6-inch square. Place a 3-inch metal ring, such as a cookie cutter, at the center of a tortilla and fold up the ends on either side of the ring opening, then clamp together with a small paper clip. Place the tortilla in a medium metal bowl so the unclamped ends fold up along the sides of the bowl. Transfer the bowl with the tortilla to the oven and bake for 5 minutes, until lightly browned and crunchy. Remove from the oven and let cool until safe to handle, then remove the paper clip and ring. Repeat with the remaining tortilla squares.

3. Make the meat filling: Heat the canola oil in a large skillet over medium-high heat. Add the onion and cook until lightly browned, about 4 minutes. Add the garlic and cook for 1 minute, until fragrant. Add the ground beef and cook until the meat is browned and cooked through, about 4 minutes. Drain any excess liquid from the pan.

4. Add the ancho chile powder, cumin, coriander, paprika, black pepper, cornstarch, salt, and orange zest and stir to combine, then use a whisk to mash the beef in the pan to break up any large pieces. Remove the pan from the heat and set aside until ready to assemble the nacos.

5. Make the cheese sauce: Dice the cheese into 1-inch cubes, then add to a medium saucepan with the diced tomatoes and water. Warm over low heat until the cheese cubes have fully melted and the tomatoes are incorporated, about 5 minutes.

6. Assemble the nacos: Add ¼ cup of tortilla chips to a naco shell, followed by ½ cup of the meat filling, ¼ cup shredded lettuce, 2 tablespoons guacamole, 2 tablespoons diced tomatoes, 2 tablespoons pickled jalapeños, 1 tablespoon sour cream, and ¼ cup cheese sauce. Repeat with the remaining ingredients to make 4 nacos total.

7. Serve immediately.

8. Enjoy!

Banana Cue

Ingredients

for 6 servings

- 3 cups avocado oil(720 mL), for frying
- 6 ripe saba bananas, peeled
- ½ cup brown sugar(100 g), packed

SPECIAL EQUIPMENT

- 6 bamboo skewers, 8 in (20 cm)

Preparation

1. Heat the avocado oil in a large diameter wok or skillet over medium-high heat until the temperature reaches 350°F (180°C).

2. Carefully add the bananas to the hot oil, then sprinkle the brown sugar over the bananas. Fry for 2 minutes without stirring to allow the sugar to caramelize. Carefully turn bananas with tongs or a wok spatula to coat with the caramelized sugar. Continue frying, turning frequently, until the bananas are deep golden brown in color, 3–5 minutes.

3. Remove the bananas from the oil and place on parchment paper and let sit until cool enough to touch, about 5 minutes.

4. Insert 1–2 skewers into the bottom of each banana cue. Serve immediately.

Street Corn Empanadas

Ingredients

for 4 servings

STREET CORN

- 1 package frozen fire-roasted corn, thawed
- ½ cup red bell pepper(50 g), finely diced
- ½ cup orange bell pepper(50 g), finely diced
- ¼ cup jalapeño(35 g), finely diced, seeded
- ¼ cup red onion(35 g), finely diced
- ¼ cup fresh cilantro leaves(10 g), chopped

- ⅓ cup crumbled cotija cheese(40 g)

- ¼ cup mayonnaise(60 g)

- 1 lime, juiced

- 2 teaspoons kosher salt

- 1 teaspoon freshly ground black pepper

- ½ teaspoon red pepper flakes

- ½ teaspoon ground cumin

- 1 egg yolk

- 2 teaspoons whole milk

ASSEMBLY

- 2 cans Pillsbury™ Original Crescent Rolls, 8 ounce (225 g)

- ¼ cup crema(60 g), plus more for dipping

- ¼ cup crumbled cotija cheese(40 g)

- 2 tablespoons fresh cilantro leaves, chopped

Preparation

1. Preheat the air fryer to 350°F (180°C).

2. Make the street corn: In a large bowl, mix together the corn, red bell pepper, orange bell pepper, jalapeño, red onion, cilantro, Cotija cheese, mayonnaise, lime juice, salt, black pepper, red pepper flakes, and cumin until well combined.

3. Assemble the empanadas: Open and unroll one can of Pillsbury™ Original Crescent Rolls. Cut into 4 rectangles, then firmly press the perforated lines together to seal. Cut each rectangle in half to form 8 squares.

4. Scoop a heaping tablespoon of the street corn filling onto the center of each square and fold the dough over the filling to form a triangle. Firmly press the edges together with a fork to seal. Repeat with the remaining dough and filling.

5. In a small bowl, whisk together the egg yolk and milk until smooth and brush the empanadas with the egg wash.

6. Place 2–3 empanadas at a time in the air fryer basket and air fry until golden brown, 3–5 minutes. Transfer to a plate while you repeat with the remaining empanadas.

7. Arrange the empanadas on a serving platter and top with the crema, Cotija cheese, and cilantro. Serve immediately.

8. Enjoy!

Herby Street Dog Sandwich

Ingredients

for 4 servings

CARAMELIZED ONIONS

- 4 tablespoons olive oil

- 2 large yellow onions, thinly sliced

QUICK PICKLED FRESNO CHILES

- 2 tablespoons sugar

- ¼ cup apple cider vinegar(60 mL)

- 2 Fresno chiles, thinly sliced

CUCUMBER-HERB SALAD

- ½ cup english cucumber(70 g), halved and thinly sliced

- 4 tablespoons fresh dill, roughly chopped

- 4 tablespoons fresh italian parsley, roughly chopped

- 1 tablespoon fresh oregano, roughly chopped

- 2 tablespoons fresh mint leaves, roughly chopped

- 1 spring onion, thinly sliced

- 1 tablespoon olive oil

- 1 tablespoon lemon juice

- kosher salt, to taste

- black pepper, to taste

SRIRACHA KETCHUP

- 1 tablespoon agave nectar

- 2 tablespoons ketchup

- 1 tablespoon sriracha

DIJONNAISE

- 1 tablespoon lemon juice

- 2 tablespoons dijon mustard

- 2 tablespoons mayonnaise

- kosher salt, to taste

- freshly ground black pepper, to taste

HOT DOGS

- nonstick cooking spray, for greasing

- 4 beef hot dogs, split lengthwise down the center with one long side left intact

- 1 package hawaiian sweet roll

- 1 tablespoon olive oil

FOR SERVING

- chip

- pickle

Preparation

1. Make the caramelized onions: Heat the olive oil in a large, heavy-bottomed pot over medium heat. Add the onions and reduce the heat to low. Allow to caramelize, stirring frequently, for 30 minutes, or until deep in color. Remove the pot from the heat.

2. Make the quick-pickled Fresno chiles: In a small bowl, mix together the sugar and apple cider vinegar. Add the Fresno chiles, then set aside until ready to serve.

3. Make the cucumber-herb salad: In a medium bowl, toss together the cucumber, dill, parsley, oregano, mint, spring onion, olive oil, and lemon juice. Season with salt and pepper to taste.

4. Make the Sriracha ketchup: In a small bowl, stir together the agave, Sriracha, and ketchup.

5. Make the Dijonnaise: In a small bowl, stir together the lemon juice, Dijon, and mayonnaise. Season with salt and pepper to taste.

6. Make the hot dogs: Preheat the broiler to high.

7. Heat a grill pan over medium heat and grease with nonstick spray. When the pan is hot, add the butterflied hot dogs, flat-side down. Place a grill weight (or a few plates) on top to keep them flat. Cook until beginning to crisp around the edges and grill marks appear, 4–6 minutes.

8. Carefully cut or tear the Hawaiian rolls into 4 rows of 2–3 rolls each. Split the Hawaiian rolls lengthwise with a bread knife, keeping a long side intact. Brush with the olive oil and place, cut-side up, on a baking sheet.

9. Turn the broiler on high, then broil the rolls until golden brown, about 3 minutes.

10. Lay a hot dog atop a toasted roll and top with some of the cucumber herb salad, caramelized onions, Sriracha ketchup, and Dijonnaise. Finish with a few pickled chiles. Repeat with the remaining ingredients.

11. Enjoy!

Watermelon Pistachio Salad

Ingredients

for 6 servings

- 6 cups red watermelon(840 g), cubed

- 5 fresh basil leaves, chopped

- 10 fresh mint leaves, chopped

- ⅓ cup lightly salted pistachios(40 g), chopped
- ¼ cup crumbled feta cheese(30 g)
- 1 teaspoon lemon zest
- 1 teaspoon orange zest

DRESSING

- 1 orange, juiced
- 1 lemon, juiced
- 1 teaspoon olive oil
- 1 tablespoon honey
- freshly ground black pepper, to taste
- kosher salt, to taste

FOR TOPPING

- 6 teaspoons balsamic glaze

Preparation

1. In a large bowl, combine the watermelon, basil, mint, pistachios, feta, lemon zest, and orange zest.

2. Make the dressing: In a small bowl, whisk together the orange juice, lemon juice, olive oil, honey, pepper, and salt until evenly combined.

3. Pour the dressing over the watermelon salad and toss gently until well-coated.

4. Serve immediately, or refrigerate for 10 minutes to chill. Just before serving, divide the watermelon salad between serving bowls and drizzle with the balsamic glaze.

5. Enjoy!

Shrimp Summer Salad with Creamy Cilantro Dressing

Ingredients

for 4 servings

DRESSING

- ½ cup fresh cilantro(20 g), chopped

- ¼ cup sour cream (60 g)
- ¼ cup mayonnaise (60 g)
- 1 lemon, juiced
- 1 clove garlic
- 1 tablespoon nutritional yeast
- 1 tablespoon fresh chives, chopped
- 2 tablespoons water
- kosher salt, to taste
- freshly ground black pepper, to taste

SALAD

- 1 romaine lettuce heart, chopped
- ¼ medium red onion, sliced
- 1 english cucumber, diced
- 1 jalapeño, seeded and sliced

- 10 mini heirloom tomatoes, quartered

- 8 ears baby corn, cooked and chopped

- 1 mango, peeled, pitted, and diced

- 1 avocado, peeled, pitted, and diced

- 1 lb medium shrimp(425 g), peeled, deveined, and cooked

- 4 tablespoons crumbled feta cheese

- 4 teaspoons fresh chives, chopped

- kosher salt, to taste

- freshly ground black pepper, to taste

Preparation

1. Make the dressing: Add the cilantro, sour cream, mayonnaise, lemon juice, garlic, nutritional yeast, chives, and water to a blender and blend until smooth. Season with salt and pepper to taste.

2. Assemble the salad: In a large bowl, combine the romaine, red onion, cucumber, jalapeño, cherry tomatoes, baby corn, mango, and avocado. Drizzle the cilantro dressing over the salad and toss until evenly coated.

3. Divide the salad between 4 serving bowls and top with the shrimp, feta, and chives. Season with salt and pepper.

4. Any leftover salad will keep in an airtight container in the refrigerator for up to 1 day.

5. Enjoy!

Pineapple Pancetta Pasta

Ingredients

for 6 servings

- kosher salt, to taste

- ½ lb dried linguine(225 g)

- 4 oz pancetta(110 g), diced

- ½ cup pineapple(75 g), diced

- ½ medium yellow onion, diced

- 3 cloves garlic, minced

- 1 tablespoon tomato paste

- 1 tablespoon olive oil

- 1 can crushed tomato

- 6 fresh basils, chopped

- ¼ teaspoon dried oregano

- ½ teaspoon dried parsley

- freshly ground black pepper, to taste

- freshly grated parmesan cheese, for serving

Preparation

1. Bring a large pot of salted water to a boil. Add the linguine and cook according to the package **instructions** until al dente, then drain, reserving ⅓ cup of the pasta cooking water.

2. Add the pancetta and pineapple to a large skillet. Cook over medium heat until the pineapple begins to char, 2–3 minutes. Transfer to a bowl and set aside.

3. Reduce the heat to low, add the onion and garlic to the skillet, and cook until golden, 2–3 minutes.

4. Add the tomato paste and olive oil and stir until evenly incorporated, then add the crushed tomatoes. Stir the sauce for 2–3 minutes, until smooth and warmed through. Cover and simmer for 2–3 minutes more, then stir in the basil, oregano, and parsley and season with salt and pepper.

5. Add the cooked pasta to the sauce and toss to coat. If the sauce is too thick, add some of the reserved pasta water.

6. Divide the pasta between bowls and top with the pineapple-pancetta mixture and freshly grated Parmesan cheese. Serve immediately.

7. Any leftovers will keep in an airtight container in the refrigerator for up to 5 days.

8. Enjoy!

Dorm-Friendly Microwave Meals For A Day

Ingredients

for 1 serving

BLUEBERRY RICOTTA CAKE

- ⅓ cup ricotta cheese(85 g)

- 3 tablespoons maple syrup

- 2 tablespoons unsalted butter, melted

- 2 tablespoons milk, of choice

- 1 large egg

- ¼ cup all-purpose flour(30 g)

- ¼ teaspoon baking powder

- 1 pinch kosher salt

- ¼ cup fresh blueberries(35 g), plus more for garnish if desired

- powdered sugar, for garnish

STREUSEL TOPPING

- 1 ½ tablespoons all-purpose flour

- 2 tablespoons brown sugar

- ⅛ teaspoon ground cinnamon

- 1 tablespoon unsalted butter, cubed and chilled

MICROWAVE CHICKEN QUESADILLA

- 2 flour tortillas, 6-inch

- ½ cup chicken strips(60 g), or shredded chicken (cooked)

- ½ bell pepper, diced

- 1 tablespoon taco seasoning

- ½ cup shredded cheddar cheese(50 g)

MICROWAVE MEAL-PREP LASAGNA

- ½ cup ricotta cheese(125 g)

- ¼ cup fresh spinach(10 g), chopped

- 2 tablespoons grated parmesan cheese, divided

- ½ teaspoon kosher salt

- ¼ teaspoon freshly ground black pepper

- ⅓ cup marinara sauce(85 g)

- 4 no-boil lasagna noodles, broken in half

- ½ cup shredded mozzarella cheese(50 g)

MICROWAVE CHEESECAKE

- 1 tablespoon unsalted butter

- 2 sheets graham cracker, crushed

- 4 oz cream cheese(110 g), softened

- 2 tablespoons sugar

- 3 drops vanilla extract

- 5 fresh raspberries, for serving

Preparation

1. Make the Blueberry Ricotta Cake: In a large, microwave-safe mug, whisk together the ricotta cheese, maple syrup, melted butter, milk, and egg until smooth. Add the flour, baking powder, and salt and stir with a small rubber spatula to combine. Fold in the blueberries.

2. Cover the mug and microwave on high power for 3–4 minutes, until the batter is cooked through.

3. Make the streusel topping: In a small bowl, stir together the flour, brown sugar, and cinnamon. Add the butter and use your fingertips to pinch into

the dry ingredients until evenly combined. Sprinkle the streusel over the mug cake.

4. Microwave uncovered for 60–90 seconds, until the topping is cooked through. Let the cake sit for 1 minute, then garnish with more blueberries and dust with powdered sugar, if desired, and serve.

5. Make the Chicken Quesadilla: Place the tortillas on a microwave-safe plate and microwave for 1 minute, until slightly crispy. Let cool while you microwave the chicken mixture; they will dry out a bit.

6. In a medium microwave-safe bowl, mix together the chicken, bell pepper, and taco seasoning until evenly combined. Microwave for 1–2 minutes, until the peppers have softened.

7. Spread the chicken mixture evenly on one tortilla, sprinkle evenly with the cheese, then top with the remaining tortilla. Microwave for 30–60 seconds, until the cheese is melted. Slice and serve immediately.

8. Make the Meal-Prep Lasagna: In a small bowl, mix together the ricotta, spinach, 1 tablespoon of Parmesan, the salt, and black pepper.

9. Spread a layer of marinara sauce on the bottom of a glass container. Arrange a layer of lasagna noodles on top. Cover the noodles with a layer of the ricotta mixture, then some of the mozzarella. Repeat to make more layers, topping the final layer of noodles with more marinara sauce, the remaining mozzarella, and the remaining tablespoon of Parmesan cheese.

10. Place the lid on top of the container, but do not seal it closed. Microwave for 7 minutes, or until the cheese is melted through. Remove from the microwave carefully, the container will be hot! Serve immediately, or let the lasagna cool and refrigerate for up to 5 days.

11. Make the Cheesecake: Melt the butter in a small microwaveable ramekin. Tilt the ramekin to coat the sides with the melted butter. Add the graham cracker crumbs to the ramekin with the melted butter and mix well. Use a spoon to press the crumbs evenly against the bottom of the dish.

12. In a small bowl, stir together the cream cheese, sugar, and vanilla until no lumps remain. Spread the filling on top of the graham cracker crust.

13. Microwave the cheesecake on half-power in 45-second increments for 4 minutes total, making sure the filling does not bubble over the sides of the ramekin. Remove the cheesecake from the microwave and chill in the freezer for at least 30 minutes, until completely cool to the touch.

14. With a knife, loosen the edges of the cheesecake, then invert onto a plate, or leave in the ramekin, and top with the raspberries before serving.

15. Enjoy!

Salmon Quinoa Bowl

Ingredients

for 2 servings

- 3 teaspoons Campbell's FlavorUp!™ Rich Garlic & Herb Cooking Concentrate, divided

- 1 ½ limes lime zest

- 1 ½ limes fresh lime juice, divided

- 4 tablespoons olive oil, divided

- 6 oz skinless salmon fillets

- ⅓ cup quinoa(60 mg)

- ⅔ cup water(160 g)

- ½ orange bell pepper orange bell pepper, diced

- ½ cup fire-roasted corn(80 g), thawed from frozen

- 1 cup cherry tomatoes(200 g), halved

- ¼ cup chopped fresh cilantro(10 g), plus more for garnish

HERB SAUCE

- ½ cup fresh cilantro leaves(20 g), finely chopped

- 1 lime lime juice

- ½ teaspoon red pepper flakes, optional

- 1 tablespoon red wine vinegar

- ¼ cup olive oil(60 mL)

- 1 teaspoon Campbell's FlavorUp!™ Rich Garlic & Herb Cooking Concentrate

Preparation

1. Preheat the oven to 350°F (180°C). Line a baking sheet with aluminum foil.

2. In a small bowl, whisk together 2 teaspoons of Campbell's FlavorUp!™ Rich Garlic & Herb Cooking Concentrate, the lime zest, juice of 1 lime, and 2 tablespoons of olive oil.

3. Place the salmon on the prepared baking sheet and pour the marinade over, coating evenly.

4. Bake the salmon until the internal temperature reaches 135°F, 20–25 minutes.

5. Meanwhile make the quinoa: In a small pot, combine the quinoa, remaining teaspoon of Campbell's FlavorUp!™ Rich Garlic & Herb Cooking Concentrate, and the water. Cook over medium heat until the water is absorbed and quinoa is tender, 5–8 minutes. Allow the quinoa to cool for 15 minutes, or until room temperature.

6. Transfer the cooled quinoa to a medium bowl. Add the remaining 2 tablespoons of olive oil, the remaining lime juice, orange bell pepper, corn, tomatoes, and cilantro and toss to combine.

7. Make the herb sauce: In a small bowl, combine the cilantro, lime juice, red pepper flakes, red wine vinegar, olive oil, and Campbell's FlavorUp!™ Rich Garlic & Herb Cooking Concentrate.

8. Assemble the bowls: Divide the quinoa between 2 serving bowls and top with the baked salmon. Drizzle the herb sauce over the quinoa and salmon. Serve warm.

9. Enjoy!

Copycat Costco Bulgogi Bake

Ingredients

for 4 servings

BULGOGI

- 1 ¼ lb boneless ribeye steak(530 g), thinly sliced

- 1 ½ tablespoons brown sugar

- 1 ½ tablespoons sesame oil

- 2 tablespoons scallions, chopped

- 3 tablespoons soy sauce, preferably Sempio Brand

- 2 tablespoons garlic, finely grated

- ¼ medium white onion, grated

- 1 ½ teaspoons fresh ginger, finely grated

- ½ meduim asian pear, grated

- 1 tablespoon gochujang

- 2 tablespoons avocado oil

ASSEMBLY

- all-purpose flour, for dusting

- 1 lb pizza dough(425 g), divided into 4 equal pieces

- 3 cups mozzarella cheese(300 g), grated, divided

- 1 ½ tablespoons avocado oil

- 2 cloves garlic, finely grated

Preparation

1. Marinate the bulgogi: add the ribeye, brown sugar, sesame oil, scallions, soy sauce, garlic, onion, ginger, Asian pear, and gochujang to a large bowl and mix until well-combined and the meat is fully coated. Marinate at room temperature for 30 minutes, or cover the bowl with plastic wrap and marinate in the refrigerator overnight.

2. Heat the avocado oil in a medium nonstick skillet over medium-high heat. Add the marinated bulgogi and cook for about 4 minutes, or until browned. Flip and cook for another 1–2 minutes, or until browned on the other side. Transfer bulgogi to a plate and let cool.

3. Assemble the bulgogi bakes: Preheat the oven to 400°F (200°C). Line a baking sheet with parchment paper.

4. Lightly dust a clean surface with flour, then use a rolling pin to roll out one portion of dough to a roughly 7 x 10-inch rectangle. Layer ¼ cup of shredded mozzarella cheese, a quarter the bulgogi, and another ¼ cup of cheese on the center of the dough, leaving a 2-inch border all the way around the edges. Fold a long side of dough up and over the fillings to the center, then repeat with the remaining long side, then the two short sides. Pinch and press the edges of the dough together to seal. Carefully transfer the bulgogi bake to the prepared baking sheet and repeat with the remaining **ingredients** to make 4 total.

5. In a small bowl, stir together the avocado oil and garlic.

6. Use a pastry brush to brush garlic oil on the tops of the bulgogi bakes, then sprinkle each with ¼ cup of mozzarella cheese.

7. Bake for 15–17 minutes, or until the cheese and dough are golden brown. Let cool for 5 minutes before serving.

8. Enjoy!

Chai-Spiced Apple Cake

Ingredients

for 8 servings

CAKE

- nonstick cooking spray, for greasing
- 1 teaspoon McCormick® Ground Cinnamon
- 1 teaspoon McCormick® ground ginger
- ½ teaspoon McCormick® Ground Nutmeg
- ¼ teaspoon McCormick® ground allspice
- ¼ teaspoon McCormick® Ground Cloves
- ¼ teaspoon McCormick Gourmet® Organic Ground Cardamom
- ½ teaspoon McCormick® ground black pepper
- 3 cups all-purpose flour(375 g)
- 2 teaspoons baking powder

- 1 teaspoon baking soda
- ½ teaspoon kosher salt
- ½ cup unsalted butter, room temperature
- ½ cup granulated sugar(100 g)
- ½ cup light brown sugar(100 g), packed
- 3 large eggs
- 1 teaspoon McCormick® All Natural Pure Vanilla Extract
- 1 ½ cups plain full-fat greek yogurt(360 mL), plain
- 3 granny smith apples, peeled, cored, and small diced

CREAM CHEESE GLAZE

- 8 oz cream cheese(225 g), softened
- ½ cup powdered sugar(55 g)
- 1 teaspoon McCormick® All Natural Pure Vanilla Extract
- ½ cup milk(120 mL), plus more as needed

Preparation

1. Preheat the oven to 375°F (190°C). Grease a Bundt pan with nonstick spray.

2. In a small bowl mix together the McCormick® Ground Cinnamon, McCormick® Ground Ginger, McCormick® Ground Nutmeg, McCormick® Ground Allspice, McCormick® Ground Cloves, and McCormick Gourmet® Organic Ground Cardamom, and McCormick® Black Pepper. Reserve ½ teaspoon of the spice mixture for garnish.

3. In a medium bowl, whisk together the flour, baking powder, baking soda, and salt.

4. In a large bowl, cream together the butter and sugar with an electric hand mixer on medium speed until light and fluffy. Add the eggs, McCormick® All Natural Pure Vanilla Extract, and Greek yogurt and mix until combined.

5. Add half of the dry ingredients to the wet ingredients and mix on low speed until incorporated Add the remaining dry ingredients and the spice mixture and mix until just combined. Fold in the diced apples with a rubber spatula.

6. Pour the batter into the prepared Bundt pan and smooth the top. Bake for 50–55 minutes, or until a toothpick inserted into the center of the cake comes out clean.

7. Meanwhile, make the cream cheese glaze: In a medium bowl, whip the cream cheese with an electric hand mixer on medium speed until light and fluffy. Add the powdered sugar, McCormick®

All Natural Pure Vanilla Extract, and milk and whip on low speed until combined. If the glaze is too thick, add more milk until it is loose enough to spread.

8. Remove the cake from the oven and let cool for 20 minutes. Flip the cake over onto a platter and spread the cream cheese glaze on top. Sprinkle the reserved spice mixture over the glaze. Let the glaze set for 10 minutes before slicing the cake and serving.

9. Enjoy!

Vegan Breakfast Lasagna

Ingredients

for 9 servings

- 3 tablespoons avocado oil

- 1 green bell pepper, julienned

- 1 yellow bell pepper, julienned

- 1 orange bell pepper, julienned

- 1 medium white onion, julienned

- 1 pack white mushroom, julienned

- 1 pack beyond sausage

- 5 yukon gold potatoes, diced

- ½ tablespoon all purpose seasoning, such as Goya

- ½ tablespoon garlic and onion powder, (or season to taste)

- 1 tablespoon smoked paprika

- 9 lasagna noodles, cooked

- ½ cup vegan butter(115 g)

- 3 tablespoons all-purpose flour

- 2 cups unsweetened plant milk(480 mL)

- ¾ cup nutritional yeast(95 g)

- 1 pack violife smoked provolone slices

- 1 bottle just egg

- 1 pack violife cheddar shreds

- Annie's biscuit, baked according to instructions

- thinly sliced chive, for garnish

Preparation

1. Sauté all the veggies, mushrooms and beyond sausage in 3 tablespoons of avocado oil until desired tenderness then place in a bowl. Using the same pan, add your diced potatoes and season to taste with Goya all-purpose seasoning, garlic and onion powder, and smoked paprika (add a little more avocado oil if necessary) sauté on low to medium heat then cover for about 10 mins.

2. Meanwhile, boil water and season it with sea salt. Once the water is ready, add your lasagna and cook to your desired tenderness.

3. In another pot on low medium heat add some vegan butter and once melted add your flour and whisk till combined. You then want to slowly whisk in your unsweetened plant milk till there's no more lumps, then add in your seasoning, nutritional yeast, and Violife cheese slices (cut into pieces.) Stir to combine, then place the lid on so the cheese can melt. You want the cheese to be smooth and creamy which will take about 10-15 minutes.

4. Once everything is cooked (veggies, beyond meat, potatoes and noodles), layer just as you would a regular lasagna: cheese sauce first, then noodles, then a little of your veggies, potatoes and shredded Violife cheese along with pieces of the baked biscuits as well. Once you're at the top, finish off with any of the ingredients you have left in addition to the shredded cheese, cheese sauce and biscuits.

5. Top with diced scallions or chives and bake in a preheated oven at 325'F for 40-45 mins or until the cheese is melted.

6. Serve warm.

Filipino Sweet Spaghetti

Ingredients

for 6 servings

- 1 tablespoon kosher salt, plus more for boiling

- 1 tablespoon canola oil

- 1 ½ lb ground beef(675 g)

- 1 tablespoon freshly ground black pepper

- 2 cups water(480 mL)

- ½ medium white onion, chopped

- 4 cloves garlic, grated

- 3 red Filipino hot dogs, preferably Martin brand, sliced crosswise ½–1-inch (1.25-2.5 cm) thick

- 35 oz sweet Filipino-style spaghetti sauce(1 kg), preferably UFC brand

- ½ cup banana ketchup(120 mL), preferably Jufran brand, or to taste

- 16 oz dried spathetti(455 g)

- Freshly grated sharp cheddar cheese, Edam cheese, or Queso de Bola

Preparation

1. Bring a large pot of salted water to a boil.

2. In a medium saucepan or skillet, heat the canola oil over medium heat until shimmering. Add the ground beef, salt, pepper, and water and cook, stirring to break up the meat, until the beef is browned, about 10 minutes.

3. Move the beef to one side of the pan, then add the onion and garlic to the other side and stir until fragrant, about 3 minutes. Mix the onion in with the beef.

4. Add the hot dogs and stir to combine. Cook until warmed through

5. Stir in the spaghetti sauce and banana ketchup until well-incorporated. Bring to a simmer and cook for 10–15 minutes, until the sauce is warmed through.

6. Add the spaghetti to the boiling water and cook according to the package instructions until al dente. Drain the noodles.

7. Divide the spaghetti between serving dishes, then ladle the spaghetti sauce on top. Sprinkle the cheese on top and let melt.

8. Enjoy!

Cranberry And Sage-Stuffed Pork Tenderloin

Ingredients

for 4 servings

- ½ cup french bread(60 g), cubed

PORK TENDERLOIN

- 2 tablespoons unsalted butter, melted

- 2 tablespoons stone-ground mustard

- 2 tablespoons light brown sugar

- ¼ teaspoon McCormick® ground black pepper

- ½ teaspoon kosher salt

- 1 teaspoon McCormick® Rubbed Sage

- 2 lb pork tenderloin(910 g)

CRANBERRY SAGE STUFFING

- ½ cup dried cranberries(70 g), roughly chopped

- ½ cup red apple(60 g), finely chopped

- 1 shallot, thinly sliced

- 1 tablespoon unsalted butter, melted

- 1 ½ teaspoons McCormick® Rubbed Sage

- ½ teaspoon kosher salt

- ¼ teaspoon McCormick® ground black pepper

- ½ cup chicken broth(120 mL)

Preparation

1. Preheat the oven to 400°F (200°C). Line 2 baking sheets with parchment paper or aluminum foil.

2. Spread the cubed French bread in a single layer on a prepared baking sheet and bake for 10–15 minutes, or until golden brown. Remove from the oven and let cool.

3. Make the rub: In a small bowl, whisk together the melted butter, mustard, brown sugar, McCormick® Ground Black Pepper, salt, and McCormick® Rubbed Sage until well-combined.

4. Make the cranberry sage stuffing: In a medium bowl, toss together the dried cranberries, apple, shallot, melted butter, McCormick® Rubbed Sage, salt, McCormick® Ground Black Pepper, chicken broth, and cooled bread cubes until evenly combined.

5. Place the tenderloin between two sheets of plastic wrap and pound until it is about ½ inch thick. Rub the tenderloin on both sides with the spice mixture. Pile the stuffing on the center of the tenderloin, then roll one side of the tenderloin tightly up and over to completely encase the stuffing, securing the end with toothpicks. Wrap the tenderloin in aluminum foil and place on the remaining prepared baking sheet.

6. Bake the tenderloin for 30 minutes. Remove the aluminum foil and bake for another 10 minutes, until the tenderloin is browned and crispy on top.

7. Remove the toothpicks, slice the pork tenderloin crosswise, and serve.

8. Enjoy!

Achiote Turkey

Ingredients

for 12 servings

DRY BRINE

- ½ teaspoon whole black peppercorn

- 6 dried bay leaves

- 1 teaspoon ground oregano

- 2 oz achiote or annatto paste(55 g)

- 5 tablespoons kosher salt

- 3 small garlic cloves

TURKEY

- 12 lb turkey(5 kg), thawed, giblets removed

- ½ cup olive oil(120 mL)

- ½ orange

- ½ red onion

- ½ yellow onion

SEASONED BUTTER

- 1 orange, juiced

- 2 oz achiote or annatto paste(55 g)

- 1 lb unsalted butter, room temperature

- 1 orange, zested

- 3 cloves garlic, minced

- ¼ teaspoon ground oregano

- 1 teaspoon kosher salt

- ¼ teaspoon freshly ground black pepper

Preparation

1. Make the dry brine: Using a mortar and pestle, grind together the black peppercorns and bay leaves until finely ground. Add the oregano and achiote paste and grind to break up the achiote, then add the salt and continue grinding until incorporated .Add the garlic and grind until well-combined.

(Alternatively, add the dry brine ingredients to a coffee grinder or blender and blend until all ingredients are well-combined.)

2. Place the turkey in a large, oven-safe roasting pan and rub with the dry brine on all sides. Cover with a lid or aluminum foil and refrigerate for 8 hours.

3. Make the seasoned butter: In a small bowl, combine the orange juice and achiote paste. Let the achiote soften for 1 hour, stirring occasionally to dissolve.

4. Add the butter to a medium bowl, along with the softened achiote paste, and mix until smooth and well-incorporated. Add the orange zest, garlic, oregano, salt, and pepper and mix until evenly combined.

5. Use your hands to separate the skin from the breast, being careful not to tear the skin. Rub the inside and outside of the turkey, including under the skin, with the seasoned butter. Cover again and refrigerate for 24 hours.

6. When ready to roast the turkey, preheat the oven to 355°F (180°C).

7. Rub the outside of the turkey with olive oil to keep the butter from burning. Place the orange half and the red and yellow onion inside the turkey cavity.

8. Place the turkey in the oven, uncovered, and roast, basting every 30 minutes with the juices from the bottom of the pan, for a total of 3 hours, or until the internal temperature has reached 165°F (75°C).

9. Remove the turkey from the oven, baste one more time, then cover and let rest for 1 hour before carving.

10. Enjoy!

Achiote Wings

Ingredients

for 4 servings

MARINADE

- 3 ½ oz achiote paste(95 g)
- ¼ large white onion
- 3 cloves garlic
- 2 dried bay leaves
- 1 cup fresh orange juice(240 mL)
- ½ cup fresh lime juice(120 mL)

- 1 teaspoon kosher salt

- ½ teaspoon whole black peppercorns

- ¼ teaspoon ground cumin

- 4 lb chicken wings (1.7 kg)

WET RUB

- 3 ½ oz achiote paste (95 g)

- ¼ large white onion

- 2 cloves garlic

- ⅓ cup fresh orange juice (80 mL)

- ¼ cup fresh lime juice (60 mL)

- ½ teaspoon kosher salt

- ¼ teaspoon whole black peppercorns

PINEAPPLE CILANTRO HABANERO DRESSING

- 6 slices pineapple

- 2 habanero peppers, to taste

- 1 bunch fresh cilantro

- ⅔ cup sour cream (160 g)

- ¼ cup mayonnaise (60 g)

- ⅓ cup heavy cream (80 g)

- kosher salt, to taste

- freshly ground black pepper, to taste

- 1 lime, juiced

FOR GARNISH (OPTIONAL)

- grilled pineapple slice

- fresh cilantro

Preparation

1. Make the marinade: In a blender, combine the achiote paste, onion, garlic, bay leaves, orange juice, lime juice, salt, peppercorns, and cumin and blend on high speed until smooth.

2. Place the chicken wings in a large bowl and add the achiote marinade. Toss to coat the wings completely, then cover the bowl and marinate in the refrigerator overnight, or at least 4 hours. Rinse out the blender.

3. Make the wet rub: In the blender, combine the achiote paste, onion, garlic, orange juice, lime juice, salt, and peppercorns and blend on high speed until smooth.

4. Drain the marinade from the wings, then toss with the wet rub until well-coated. Clean the blender.

5. Preheat the grill to medium-high heat. Arrange the wings on the grill grates and cook for 30 minutes, flipping every 5 minutes, until the internal temperature reaches 165°F (75°C). Remove the wings from the grill and let rest for 5 minutes.

6. Meanwhile, make the pineapple cilantro habanero dressing: Grill the pineapple slices and habaneros for 5 minutes on each side, or until tender and grill marks appear.

7. Transfer the pineapple and habanero to the blender, along with the cilantro, sour cream, mayonnaise, heavy cream, lime juice, salt, and pepper. Blend until smooth.

8. Arrange the wings on a platter and drizzle with the dressing, or serve alongside as a dip. Garnish with more grilled pineapple and cilantro, if desired.

9. Enjoy!

Savory French Toast

Ingredients

for 6 servings

- 5 large eggs

- ½ cup heavy cream(120 mL)

- ½ teaspoon dried parsley

- ¼ teaspoon garlic powder

- ¼ teaspoon onion powder

- ½ teaspoon paprika

- kosher salt, to taste

- freshly ground black pepper, to taste

- 6 slices challah bread, 1-in (2.54-cm) thick

- unsalted butter, for cooking

TOPPINGS (OPTIONAL)

- Roasted bell pepper-flavored whipped cream cheese, such as Philadelphia brand

- quartered cherry tomato, quartered

- chopped, cooked bacon

- chopped fresh chive

- hot honey

Preparation

1. In a deep cake pan or pie dish, whisk together the eggs, heavy cream, parsley, garlic powder, onion powder, paprika, salt, and pepper until smooth.

2. Dip each slice of challah in the egg mixture for about 30 seconds per side, until the bread absorbs the egg, but is not soggy.

3. Melt a pat of butter in a large pan over medium heat. Working in batches if needed, cook the French toast until golden brown, about 2 minutes on each side.

4. Serve immediately with your toppings of choice, such as roasted red pepper cream cheese, cherry tomatoes, bacon, chives, and a drizzle of hot honey.

5. Enjoy!

Carnitas Tostadas With Pineapple Salsa

Ingredients

for 4 servings

CARNITAS

- 2 ½ lb boneless pork shoulder(1 kg), cut into 2-inch (5 cm) cubes
- 3 teaspoons kosher salt, divided
- 2 ½ teaspoons McCormick® Pure Ground Black Pepper, divided
- 2 tablespoons neutral oil, such as canola
- 1 cup chicken stock(240 mL)
- ½ cup orange juice(120 mL)

- ¼ cup lime juice(60 mL)

- 8 cloves garlic, roughly chopped

- 1.12 oz McCormick® Fajita Seasoning Mix(30 g)

- 1 teaspoon McCormick® dried oregano

PINEAPPLE SALSA

- 1 cup finely diced pineapple(140 g)

- 1 cup finely diced mango(140 g)

- ½ cup finely diced red onion(75 g)

- ½ cup finely diced red bell pepper(50 g)

- ¼ cup finely chopped jalapeño(20 g)

- 2 limes, juiced

- ½ teaspoon McCormick® Crushed Red Pepper

- 1 teaspoon kosher salt

TOSTADAS

- 8 tostadas, 8 in (20 cm)

- 1 cup guacamole (365 g)

Preparation

1. Make the carnitas: Season the pork with 2 teaspoons of salt and 2 teaspoons of McCormick® Pure Ground Black Pepper.

2. Turn the Instant Pot on the Sauté setting, then add the oil and heat until it shimmers, 1–2 minutes. Working in batches to avoid overcrowding the pot, sear the pork until golden brown, about 2 minutes on each side. Transfer the pork to a plate as it's done searing.

3. Return all of the seared pork to the Instant Pot, along with any juices that have accumulated on the plate, then add the chicken stock, orange juice, lime juice, garlic, McCormick® Fajita Spice Mix, McCormick® Dried Oregano, the remaining teaspoon of salt, and the remaining ½ teaspoon of McCormick® Pure Ground Black Pepper and stir to combine. Turn off the Sauté setting, then secure the Instant Pot lid, making sure the vent is set to sealing. Manually set to cook on high pressure for 30 minutes. Once the timer goes off, let the pressure release naturally for 20 minutes, then carefully switch the vent to release the rest of the steam.

4. Make the pineapple salsa: In a medium bowl, combine the pineapple, mango, red onion, red bell pepper, jalapeño, lime juice, McCormick® Crushed Red Pepper, and salt. Refrigerate until ready to serve.

5. Turn the broiler on high. Line a baking sheet with aluminum foil.

6. Uncover the Instant Pot, then use a slotted spoon to transfer the pork to the prepared baking sheet, leaving the liquid behind in the pot. Shred the pork with two forks, then add ½ cup (120 ml) of the liquid from the pot and toss to moisten the pork.

7. Broil the pork for 3–5 minutes, or until the top is crispy. Remove the baking sheet from the broiler and toss, then broil again for 3–5 minutes more, or until very crispy. Remove from the oven.

8. Assemble the tostadas: Spread 1–2 tablespoons of guacamole on each tostada, then top with the carnitas and pineapple salsa.

9. Serve warm.

10. Enjoy!

Vanessa's Nicaraguan Carne Asada With Queso Frito

Ingredients

for 4 servings

CARNE ASADA

- ½ cup bitter orange juice(120 mL), such as Goya Bitter Orange Marinade, or 6 tablespoons orange juice plus 2 tablespoons lemon juice

- 1 tablespoon worcestershire sauce

- 1 teaspoon adobo seasoning, preferably Goya

- ½ teaspoon freshly ground black pepper

- 2 lb skirt steak(910 g), cut into 1-inch (2.5-cm)-wide strips

- 2 tablespoons vegetable oil

QUESO FRITO

- 10 oz frying cheese(280 g), such as El Latino Queso Freir, cut into ½-inch (1.2-cm)-thick slices

- canola oil, for frying

FRIED PLANTAINS

- 2 ripe plantains

- canola oil, for frying

- kosher salt, to taste

FOR SERVING

• rice and bean

• milca soda

Preparation

1. Make the carne asada: In a medium bowl, combine the orange juice, Worcestershire sauce, adobo seasoning, black pepper, and skirt steak. Stir to coat the steak well. Cover the bowl and marinate in the refrigerator for at least 8 hours, up to 24 hours

2. Heat a grill pan over medium-high heat until smoking. Add 1 tablespoon of vegetable oil, then, working in batches to avoid overcrowding the pan, add the steak and sear on one side for 2–3 minutes, until grill marks appear. Flip and cook for another 2–4 minutes, depending on desired doneness (2 minutes for medium-rare, 3–4 minutes for medium-well). Repeat with the remaining steak, greasing the grill pan with more vegetable oil as needed. Transfer the steak to a cutting board and let rest for 5–10 minutes before serving.

3. Make the queso frito: Fill a large skillet with ⅛ inch (3 mm) of canola oil and heat over medium heat until the temperature reaches 350°F (180°C).

4. Working in batches if needed to avoid overcrowding the pan, fry the cheese in the hot oil for 1–2 minutes per side, until golden brown. Transfer to a paper towel-lined plate to drain.

5. Make the fried plantains: Trim the ends of the plantains, then peel and slice on the bias into ½-inch (1.3 cm)-thick pieces.

6. Add more oil to the same skillet if needed to reach a depth of ⅛ inch (3 mm). Heat over medium-high heat until the temperature reaches 350°F (180°C)..

7. Working in batches to avoid overcrowding the pan, add the plantains to the hot oil and fry until golden brown, 2–3 minutes per side. Transfer to a paper towel-lined plate and season with salt.

8. Serve the carne asada, queso frito, and plantains with rice and beans and Milca sodas.

9. Enjoy!

Carnitas Tostadas With Pineapple Salsa

Ingredients

for 4 servings

CARNITAS

- 2 ½ lb boneless pork shoulder(1 kg), cut into 2-inch (5 cm) cubes

- 3 teaspoons kosher salt, divided

- 2 ½ teaspoons McCormick® Pure Ground Black Pepper, divided

- 2 tablespoons neutral oil, such as canola

- 1 cup chicken stock(240 mL)

- ½ cup orange juice(120 mL)

- ¼ cup lime juice(60 mL)

- 8 cloves garlic, roughly chopped

- 1.12 oz McCormick® Fajita Seasoning Mix(30 g)

- 1 teaspoon McCormick® dried oregano

PINEAPPLE SALSA

- 1 cup finely diced pineapple(140 g)

- 1 cup finely diced mango(140 g)

- ½ cup finely diced red onion(75 g)

- ½ cup finely diced red bell pepper(50 g)

- ¼ cup finely chopped jalapeño(20 g)

- 2 limes, juiced

- ½ teaspoon McCormick® Crushed Red Pepper

- 1 teaspoon kosher salt

TOSTADAS

- 8 tostadas, 8 in (20 cm)

- 1 cup guacamole(365 g)

Preparation

1. Make the carnitas: Season the pork with 2 teaspoons of salt and 2 teaspoons of McCormick® Pure Ground Black Pepper.

2. Turn the Instant Pot on the Sauté setting, then add the oil and heat until it shimmers, 1–2 minutes. Working in batches to avoid overcrowding the pot, sear the pork until golden brown, about 2 minutes on each side. Transfer the pork to a plate as it's done searing.

3. Return all of the seared pork to the Instant Pot, along with any juices that have accumulated on the plate, then add the chicken stock, orange juice, lime

juice, garlic, McCormick® Fajita Spice Mix, McCormick® Dried Oregano, the remaining teaspoon of salt, and the remaining ½ teaspoon of McCormick® Pure Ground Black Pepper and stir to combine. Turn off the Sauté setting, then secure the Instant Pot lid, making sure the vent is set to sealing. Manually set to cook on high pressure for 30 minutes. Once the timer goes off, let the pressure release naturally for 20 minutes, then carefully switch the vent to release the rest of the steam.

4. Make the pineapple salsa: In a medium bowl, combine the pineapple, mango, red onion, red bell pepper, jalapeño, lime juice, McCormick® Crushed Red Pepper, and salt. Refrigerate until ready to serve.

5. Turn the broiler on high. Line a baking sheet with aluminum foil.

6. Uncover the Instant Pot, then use a slotted spoon to transfer the pork to the prepared baking sheet, leaving the liquid behind in the pot. Shred the pork with two forks, then add ½ cup (120 ml) of the liquid from the pot and toss to moisten the pork.

7. Broil the pork for 3–5 minutes, or until the top is crispy. Remove the baking sheet from the broiler and toss, then broil again for 3–5 minutes more, or until very crispy. Remove from the oven.

8. Assemble the tostadas: Spread 1–2 tablespoons of guacamole on each tostada, then top with the carnitas and pineapple salsa.

9. Serve warm.

10. Enjoy!

DESSERTS RECIPES FOR BIPOLAR DISORDER

Cardamom-Spiced Carrot Cupcakes

Ingredients

for 24 cupcakes

CUPCAKE BATTER

- 3 carrots, quartered

- 1 stick unsalted butter, room temperature

- 1 cup granulated sugar(200 g)

- 1 cup light brown sugar(200 g), packed

- 3 large eggs, room temperature

- 2 teaspoons vanilla extract

- 2 cups all purpose flour(150 g)

- 2 teaspoons baking powder

- 2 teaspoons baking soda
- ½ teaspoon kosher salt
- 2 teaspoons ground cinnamon
- ¼ teaspoon ground ginger
- ¼ teaspoon ground nutmeg
- 1 cup coconut oil(240 mL), melted
- 2 tablespoons ground cardamom, plus 1 teaspoon
- 2 ⅓ cups Fisher® Chef's Naturals Pecan Halves(233 g), finely chopped, divided

ORANGE, CARDAMOM, AND GINGER-SPICED CREAM CHEESE FROSTING

- 10 oz cream cheese(300 g), room temperature
- 2 teaspoons vanilla extract
- 4 cups powdered sugar(440 g)
- 1 orange, zested

- 1 teaspoon ground cardamom

- ½ teaspoon ground ginger

Preparation

1. Preheat the oven to 350°F (180°C). Line 2 12-cup muffin tins with paper liners and grease with butter spray.

2. Make the base carrot cupcake batter: In a food processor, process the carrots until finely chopped.

3. In a large bowl, whip the butter with an electric hand mixer on medium speed until fluffy, about 2 minutes. Add the granulated and brown sugars, and beat until smooth, about 2 minutes, scraping down the sides of the bowl as needed.

4. In a small bowl, beat together the eggs and vanilla extract.

5. Add the egg mixture to the butter mixture in thirds, beating on medium speed between each addition until fully incorporated.

6. In a medium bowl, combine the flour, baking powder, baking soda, salt, cinnamon, ginger, and nutmeg.

7. Add the dry ingredients to the wet ingredients in thirds, beating on low speed between each addition until incorporated.

8. Add the coconut oil and beat on medium-low speed for 1 minute, until fluffy.

9. Finish making the cupcakes according to your desired variation.

10. For the Cardamom-Spiced Carrot Cupcakes: When making the batter, add the cardamom to the dry ingredients. Gently fold in the carrots and 1⅓ cups Fisher Pecans. Divide the batter evenly between the prepared muffin cups, filling each about ¾ of the way full. Bake the cupcakes for 15–17 minutes, or until a toothpick inserted into the center of a cupcake comes out clean. Remove the cupcakes from the oven and let cool completely before frosting.

11. Meanwhile, make the orange, cardamom, and ginger-spiced cream cheese frosting: In a large bowl, whip together the cream cheese and vanilla extract with an electric hand mixer on medium speed until fluffy, 2 minutes, scraping down the sides of the bowl as needed. Add the powdered sugar and beat on low speed until smooth. Add the orange zest, cardamom, and ginger, and beat until incorporated. Transfer the frosting to a piping bag fitted with a large round tip. Refrigerate until ready to use.

12. To frost, place the tip of the piping bag upright at the center of a cupcake and squeeze until the cupcake is covered with frosting. Repeat with the remaining cupcakes, then garnish the edges with the remaining cup of Fisher Pecans.

13. Enjoy!

Healthy ABC Pudding

Ingredients

for 2 servings

• 2 ripe bananas, sliced

• 1 small avocado, ripe but not mushy, diced

• ¼ cup unsweetened cacao powder(25 g)

• ½ teaspoon vanilla extract

• 4 teaspoons maple syrup

• 1 pinch kosher salt

TOPPING IDEAS

• chocolate chip

• mixed berry

- toasted coconut flake

- toasted nut

- cacao nib

- banana, sliced

- granola

Preparation

1. Add the banana and avocado to the bowl of a food processor and process until completely smooth. Scrape down the sides of the bowl, then add the cacao powder, vanilla, maple syrup, and salt. Blend until smooth and the color is the same throughout.

2. Transfer the pudding to a bowl, cover with plastic wrap, and refrigerate for 15–30 minutes.

3. When ready to serve, divide the pudding between 2 serving bowls and top with your favorite toppings, such as chocolate chips, berries, toasted coconut flakes, toasted nuts, cacao nibs, sliced banana, and/or granola.

4. Enjoy!

Citrusy Squash Smash Cake

Ingredients

for 12 cupcakes

- ⅓ cup squash(65 g), shredded

- ⅓ cup applesauce(75 g)

- 1 banana, small

- ⅓ cup coconut sugar(65 g), optional

- 2 teaspoons orange zest

- 2 teaspoons vanilla extract

- 1 ½ cups all purpose flour(185 g)

- 1 ½ teaspoons baking powder

- ⅛ teaspoon ground cardamom

- ⅛ teaspoon salt

Preparation

1. Preheat the oven to 350°F.

2. Grease the muffin tin with your favorite neutral cooking oil then line with parchment cups or paper. Place on a sheet tray.

3. Mix the squash, applesauce, banana, coconut yogurt, coconut oil, orange zest, vanilla extract, and coconut sugar if you're using it. Use a fork to mash the banana then stir to thoroughly combine all the ingredients.

4. In a separate mixing bowl, whisk together the flour, baking powder, cardamom, and salt.

5. Add the dry ingredients to the bowl with the wet ingredients. Use a spatula to stir until combined and no streaks of flour remain.

6. Evenly distribute the batter in the muffin tins, filling about halfway to leave enough room for the cakes to rise without spilling over the edge of the pan. Use the spatula to smooth the tops and push the batter into the edges of the muffin liners.

7. Bake until a toothpick inserted in the center of the cupcakes comes out clean, about 25 minutes.

8. Cool and serve!

Hamster Cupcakes

Ingredients

for 12 cupcakes

• 3 ¾ cups cream cheese frosting(430 g), divided

• 12 carrot cake cupcakes

• 1 drop pink food coloring

• 3 drops orange food coloring

• 24 white chocolate melting wafers

• 12 mini marshmallows, halved lengthwise

• 24 black jumbo nonpareils

Preparation

1. Add ¾ cup (165 grams) cream cheese frosting to a piping bag fitted with a star tip.

2. In a small bowl, mix 3 tablespoons of cream cheese frosting with the pink food coloring, then transfer to a small piping bag fitted with a small round tip.

3. Add the remaining cream cheese frosting to a medium bowl and mix with the orange food coloring until the desired shade of orange is reached. Transfer to a large piping bag fitted with a star tip.

4. Holding the piping bag upright, pipe the orange frosting in a circle around the edge of a cupcake, then fill in the center. Pipe 2 slightly larger mounds of frosting on the top corners of the cupcake as ears.

5. Place 2 white chocolate wafers adjacent to each other at the bottom center of the cupcake, then nestle 2 mini marshmallow halves slightly under the space where the wafers meet as hamster teeth. Using the white cream cheese frosting, pipe a dime-sized mound where the 2 wafers meet and a small dot in the center of each ear. Pipe a dot of pink frosting on top of the white mound as the nose. Place 2 nonpareils above the wafers as eyes. Repeat with the remaining cupcakes.

6. Refrigerate until ready to serve.

7. Enjoy!

Butter Beer

Ingredients

for 4 servings

BUTTERSCOTCH SYRUP

- ⅓ cup unsalted butter(75 g)

- 1 ½ cups dark brown sugar(300 g)

- ⅓ cup light corn syrup(110 g)

- ⅔ cup heavy cream(160 g)

- 1 teaspoon kosher salt

- 1 teaspoon apple cider vinegar

- ½ teaspoon rum extract

- ½ teaspoon vanilla extract

WHIPPED TOPPING

- 1 cup heavy cream (240 mL)

- 1 oz marshmallow fluff (30 g)

- ½ teaspoon rum extract

ASSEMBLY

- 3 cans cream soda

Preparation

1. Make the butterscotch syrup: In a medium pot fitted with a candy thermometer, combine the butter, brown sugar, and corn syrup. Cook over medium-high heat, stirring occasionally, until the temperature reaches 240°F (115°C). Remove the pot from the heat and let cool for 5 minutes.

2. Stir in the heavy cream until well combined, then stir in the salt, apple cider vinegar, rum extract, and vanilla until well incorporated. Transfer to an airtight container and set aside at room temperature until ready to use.

3. Make the whipped topping: Add the heavy cream, marshmallow fluff, 2 tablespoons of butterscotch syrup, and the rum extract to a large liquid measuring cup or medium bowl. Using an immersion blender, whip until soft peaks form, 2–3 minutes.

4. Assemble the butter beer: In a large pitcher, stir together 3 tablespoons butterscotch syrup and ½ cup cream soda until well combined. Stir in the remaining cream soda.

5. Divide the butter beer between glasses and top with the whipped topping and more butterscotch syrup, if desired.

6. Enjoy!

Stove-Top Cinnamon Apples

Ingredients

for 6 servings

- 2 lb apple(1 kg), (Golden / Ginger gold / Canada / Boskoop / Fuji)

- ½ cup water(100 mL)

- ½ teaspoon lemon juice

- ½ teaspoon ginger, peeled and grated

- 1 teaspoon cinnamon

- ½ teaspoon pepper

- 1 teaspoon raw honey

Preparation

1. Peel the apples, remove the core, and cut the apples into small equal pieces. Put the apple pieces in a pot and add water

2. Add all the other ingredients Lemon juice, cinnamon, pepper, and ginger. Simmer for 2 minutes at high flame while gently mixing all the ingredients with a wooden spoon.

3. Cover it and reduce the flame to medium for 5 minutes to bring to a boil.

4. Uncover it, add honey, then gently mix again with the wooden spoon, cover it and simmer on low flame for 20 minutes. Cook until you get a soft texture. Add 5 minutes if necessary.

5. Serve warm and/or store.

Pistachio-Orange Thumbprint Cookies with Chocolate Ganache

Ingredients

for 30 cookies

- 1 cup raw pistachios(125 g), plus more for garnish

- 1 cup all purpose flour(125 g), plus 2 tablespoons

- ¾ teaspoon kosher salt

- ¾ teaspoon baking powder

- 1 ¼ sticks unsalted butter, room temperature

- ½ cup sugar(100 g)

- 1 large egg, room temperature

- 2 teaspoons orange zest

- 6 oz semi-sweet chocolate chips(165 g), roughly chopped

- ½ cup heavy cream(120 mL)

- 1 teaspoon light corn syrup

Preparation

1. Line 2 baking sheets with parchment paper.

2. Add the pistachios to the bowl of a food processor and process until ground into a slightly coarse, but even crumb (it should resemble almond flour and hold together briefly when pressed between your fingers). Measure out ¾ cup plus 2 tablespoons of the ground pistachio and transfer to a medium bowl, reserving the remaining 2 tablespoons for garnish.

3. Add the flour, salt, and baking powder to the bowl with the ground pistachios and whisk to combine.

4. In a large bowl, cream together the butter and sugar with an electric mixer on medium speed until light and fluffy, 1–2 minutes. Add the egg and orange zest and beat until evenly distributed.

5. Add the dry ingredients to the butter mixture in 3 additions, mixing after each addition until just incorporated. Finish bringing the dough together with your hands, if needed.

6. Use a ½-ounce scoop, portion the dough onto the prepared baking sheets, spacing 2 inches apart. Press the tip of your thumb or the back of a wooden spoon into the center of each cookie to create a deep well, being careful not to press through the cookie entirely. Lightly cover with plastic wrap and transfer to the freezer for 30 minutes, or refrigerate for about 1 hour, until firm.

7. Arrange the racks in the center of the oven. Preheat the oven to 350°F (180°C).

8. Bake the cookies for 14–16 minutes, turning once halfway through, until puffed and golden on the bottoms. The thumbprints will lose some of their definition during baking, so use the back of a teaspoon measure to press into indentation immediately after removing from the oven, then let cool completely, about 20 minutes.

9. While the cookies cool, make the ganache: Add the chocolate to a medium bowl. Microwave the cream on medium power for 45–60 seconds, until just steaming. Pour the hot cream over the chocolate and let sit for 1–2 minutes to give the chocolate time to melt. Add the corn syrup, if using, then whisk until completely smooth. Transfer the ganache to a piping bag or zip-top bag.

10. Once the cookies have cooled, pipe (or spoon) about 1½ teaspoons of ganache into each thumbprint. Alternatively, use a teaspoon to spoon the ganache onto the cookies. Garnish each cookie with the reserved pistachio flour or a single whole pistachio, if desired. Let the ganache set for about 30 minutes before serving.

11. Enjoy!

Alix And Zoya's Pride Party

Ingredients

for 6 servings

ALIX'S EASY BANANA DONUTS

- 6 cups canola oil(1.4 L), for frying
- 2 ripe bananas, peeled and mashed
- 1 cup whole-milk vanilla yogurt(240 mL)
- ¼ cup granulated sugar(50 g)
- 2 ½ cups self-rising flour(315 g), plus more for dusting

FOR DECORATING

- cream cheese frosting
- rainbow sprinkle

ZOYA'S SPICED EGGPLANT WRAPS

- 2 large eggplants, cut into ¼-inch (6 mm)-thick rounds
- 1 teaspoon kosher salt, plus more to taste
- ½ teaspoon freshly ground black pepper
- 1 teaspoon garlic powder

- 1 teaspoon ground turmeric

- 1 teaspoon paprika

- 2 tablespoons olive oil, plus more as needed

- 6 pieces pita bread

- 1 cup hummus(250 g)

- 1 cup greek yogurt(245 g)

- 3 roma tomatoes, sliced

- 3 Radishes, thinly sliced

- ½ cup fresh basil leaves(20 g)

- ½ cup fresh mint leaf(20 g)

- ½ cup fresh dill(20 g), torn

ZOYA'S SHIRAZI SALAD

- 2 cups persian cucumber(240 g), finely chopped

- 1 ½ cups large roma tomatoes(300 g), finely chopped

- 1 cup large red onion(150 g), finely chopped

- 2 tablespoons dried mint

- 4 tablespoons lime, juiced

- 2 tablespoons olive oil

- 2 teaspoons kosher salt, plus more to taste

- 1 teaspoon freshly ground black pepper

Preparation

1. Make Alix's Easy Banana Donuts: Add the canola oil to a large Dutch oven and heat over medium-high heat until the temperature reaches 350°F (180°C).

2. In a large bowl, whisk together the bananas, yogurt, milk, and sugar. Stir in the flour until just combined.

3. Turn the dough out onto a floured surface and knead for about 1 minute, until all the flour has been incorporated.

4. Roll the dough into 2-tablespoons balls; you should have about 24.

5. Working in batches to avoid overcrowding the pot, fry the donuts in the hot oil until golden brown and cooked through, 3–4 minutes. Use a slotted

spoon to transfer to a paper towel-lined plate to drain. Repeat with the remaining donuts.

6. Let the donuts cool slightly, then spread a bit of cream cheese frosting on top of each and garnish with rainbow sprinkles.

7. Make Zoya's Spiced Eggplant Wraps: Season the eggplant slices on both sides with salt. Let sit for 5 minutes, until moisture begins to appear on the surface.

8. In a small bowl, whisk together 1 teaspoon kosher salt, ½ teaspoon black pepper, the garlic powder, turmeric, and paprika.

9. Blot the eggplant slices of excess water with paper towels, then season on both sides with the spice mixture.

10. Heat 2 tablespoons of olive oil in a large nonstick skillet over medium heat. Working in batches, add the eggplant slices in a single layer and cook until browned and tender, 3–4 minutes per side. Repeat with the remaining eggplant slices, adding more oil as needed.

11. To assemble the wraps, spread a few tablespoons of hummus and labne over a piece of lavash bread. Top with some of the grilled eggplant, tomato, radish, basil, mint, and dill. Tightly wrap up. Repeat with the remaining ingredients to make 6 wraps total.

12. Make Zoya's Shirazi Salad: In a large bowl, toss together the cucumbers, tomatoes, red onion, mint, lime juice, olive oil, salt, and pepper until well-combined. Season with more salt and pepper to taste.

13. Serve immediately.

14. Enjoy!

Chai-Spiced Apple Cake

Ingredients

for 8 servings

CAKE

- nonstick cooking spray, for greasing

- 1 teaspoon McCormick® Ground Cinnamon

- 1 teaspoon McCormick® ground ginger

- ½ teaspoon McCormick® Ground Nutmeg

- ¼ teaspoon McCormick® ground allspice

- ¼ teaspoon McCormick® Ground Cloves

- ¼ teaspoon McCormick Gourmet® Organic Ground Cardamom

- ½ teaspoon McCormick® ground black pepper

- 3 cups all-purpose flour(375 g)

- 2 teaspoons baking powder

- 1 teaspoon baking soda

- ½ teaspoon kosher salt

- ½ cup unsalted butter, room temperature

- ½ cup granulated sugar(100 g)

- ½ cup light brown sugar(100 g), packed

- 3 large eggs

- 1 teaspoon McCormick® All Natural Pure Vanilla Extract

- 1 ½ cups plain full-fat greek yogurt(360 mL), plain

- 3 granny smith apples, peeled, cored, and small diced

CREAM CHEESE GLAZE

- 8 oz cream cheese(225 g), softened

- ½ cup powdered sugar(55 g)

- 1 teaspoon McCormick® All Natural Pure Vanilla Extract

- ½ cup milk(120 mL), plus more as needed

Preparation

1. Preheat the oven to 375°F (190°C). Grease a Bundt pan with nonstick spray.

2. In a small bowl mix together the McCormick® Ground Cinnamon, McCormick® Ground Ginger, McCormick® Ground Nutmeg, McCormick® Ground Allspice, McCormick® Ground Cloves, and McCormick Gourmet® Organic Ground Cardamom, and McCormick® Black Pepper. Reserve ½ teaspoon of the spice mixture for garnish.

3. In a medium bowl, whisk together the flour, baking powder, baking soda, and salt.

4. In a large bowl, cream together the butter and sugar with an electric hand mixer on medium speed until light and fluffy. Add the eggs, McCormick® All Natural Pure Vanilla Extract, and Greek yogurt and mix until combined.

5. Add half of the dry ingredients to the wet ingredients and mix on low speed until incorporated Add the remaining dry ingredients and the spice mixture and mix until just combined. Fold in the diced apples with a rubber spatula.

6. Pour the batter into the prepared Bundt pan and smooth the top. Bake for 50–55 minutes, or until a toothpick inserted into the center of the cake comes out clean.

7. Meanwhile, make the cream cheese glaze: In a medium bowl, whip the cream cheese with an electric hand mixer on medium speed until light and fluffy. Add the powdered sugar, McCormick® All Natural Pure Vanilla Extract, and milk and whip on low speed until combined. If the glaze is too thick, add more milk until it is loose enough to spread.

8. Remove the cake from the oven and let cool for 20 minutes. Flip the cake over onto a platter and spread the cream cheese glaze on top. Sprinkle the reserved spice mixture over the glaze. Let the glaze set for 10 minutes before slicing the cake and serving.

9. Enjoy!

Ice Spice-Inspired Orange Caramel

Ingredients

for 4 servings

- ¼ cup water (60 mL)
- 1 cup granulated sugar (200 g)
- ¼ cup fresh orange juice (60 mL)
- 1 tablespoon salted butter
- ½ cup heavy cream (120 mL)
- 1 teaspoon vanilla bean paste
- ¼ teaspoon allspice
- ½ teaspoon cayenne pepper
- ¼ teaspoon sea salt
- vanilla ice cream, for serving (optional)
- chopped walnut, for garnish (optional)
- orange zest, for garnish (optional)

Preparation

1. In a medium saucepan, combine the water, sugar, and orange juice. Bring to a simmer over low heat. Cook, removing the pot from the heat and swirling if the bubbles begin to rise to the surface, until the mixture is reduced to a thick syrup and the color turns light brown, 20–30 minutes.

2. Remove the pot from the heat, add the butter, and stir immediately to combine. Add the cream, vanilla paste, allspice, cayenne, and salt and stir until incorporated and the consistency is smooth. Let cool for at least 10 minutes before using, or let cool completely before transferring to an airtight container and storing in the refrigerator until ready to use, up to 3 weeks.

3. Drizzle over ice cream and top with walnuts and orange zest, if desired, or serve with apple slices for dipping.

4. Enjoy!

Unicorn Cookies

Ingredients

for 30 cookies

- 16 tablespoons unsalted butter

- 1 cup granulated sugar(200 g)

- ⅔ cup light brown sugar(150 g), packed

- 1 tablespoon corn syrup

- 2 large eggs

- ½ teaspoon vanilla extract

- 2 cups all purpose flour(250 g)

- ½ teaspoon baking powder

- ¼ teaspoon baking soda

- 1 teaspoon kosher salt

- ¾ cup white chocolate chip(130 g)

- ½ cup rainbow sprinkles(80 g)

- ⅓ cup rolled oats(25 g)

- 1 cup sweetened rice cereal(30 g)

- 1 cup fruit shaped cereal(30 g)

- 30 cone shaped corn chips, for garnish

Preparation

1. In a large bowl with an electric hand mixer or in a stand mixer fitted with the paddle attachment, cream together the butter, granulated sugar, brown sugar, and corn syrup until light and fluffy, about 5 minutes.

2. Scrape down the sides of the bowl with a rubber spatula, then add the eggs and vanilla. Beat for 3 minutes, or until fully incorporated.

3. Add the flour, baking powder, baking soda, and salt and mix just until the dough comes together. Do not overmix.

4. Scrape down the sides of the bowl again, then fold in the white chocolate chips, sprinkles, oats, rice cereal, and fruit-shaped cereal.

5. Using an ice cream scoop or ¼ measuring cup (60 grams), scoop the dough onto a parchment-lined baking sheet. Cover with plastic wrap and refrigerate for at least 1 hour, or up to a 1 week.

6. Preheat the oven to 350°F (180°C). Line baking sheets with parchment paper.

7. Arrange the chilled dough balls 4 inches (10 cm) apart on the prepared baking sheets.

8. Bake for 6 minutes, then remove the cookies from the oven and place a corn chip in the center of each cookie to resemble a unicorn horn. Return to the oven for 6-8 minutes more, until lightly browned around the edges.

9. Let the cookies cool completely on the baking sheets before serving. The cookies will keep in an airtight container at room temperature for 5 days, or in the freezer for up to 1 month.

10. Enjoy!

Ice Cream Bombe

Ingredients

for 12 servings

3.5 qt strawberry ice cream(3.5 L), softened

VANILLA CAKE

nonstick cooking spray, for greasing

¾ cup buttermilk(180 mL)

¼ cup vegetable oil(60 mL)

1 teaspoon vanilla extract

2 cups all purpose flour(250 g), or cake flour

1 teaspoon baking powder

½ teaspoon baking soda

¾ teaspoon kosher salt

1 cup granulated sugar (200 g)

¼ cup light brown sugar (55 g), lightly packed

8 tablespoons unsalted butter, room temperature

2 large eggs

2 large egg yolks

CHOCOLATE GLAZE

12 oz dark chocolate (340 g), chopped

12 tablespoons unsalted butter

¼ cup light corn syrup (60 mL)

SPECIAL EQUIPMENT

1 tall glass bowl, 9 inch (23 cm)

offset spatula

Preparation

Line a 9-inch diameter glass bowl with enough plastic wrap to hang over the edges by 6 inches (15 ¼ cm) all the way around. You may have to use more than one piece of plastic.

Add the softened ice cream to a medium bowl. Mix with an electric hand mixer until smooth.

Transfer the softened ice cream to the prepared glass bowl and smooth the top with a rubber spatula so the ice cream is about 1½ inches (4 cm) from the rim of the bowl. Reserve any leftover ice cream in the freezer. Gently press another piece of plastic wrap over the ice cream to prevent freezer burn and freeze for at least 8 hours, up to overnight.

Make the vanilla cake: Arrange a rack in the center of the oven. Preheat the oven to 350°F (180°C). Line a 9-inch (23-cm) round cake pan with parchment paper and grease with nonstick spray.

In a liquid measuring cup or medium bowl, mix together the buttermilk, vegetable oil, and vanilla.

In a separate medium bowl, sift together the flour, baking powder, baking soda, and salt.

In a large bowl, combine the granulated sugar, brown sugar, and butter. Beat with an electric hand mixer on high speed until light and fluffy, about 4 minutes.

Add the eggs, 1 at a time, and the egg yolks, beating between each addition. Continue beating until almost doubled in volume and very light and fluffy, about 5 minutes.

With the mixer on low speed, gently beat in a third of the flour mixture. Before it's fully combined, add half of the buttermilk mixture. Repeat with another third of the flour, the remaining buttermilk mixture, and the remaining flour and mix until well-blended and no lumps remain. Pour the cake batter into the prepared pan.

Bake for 45–50 minutes, rotating the pan halfway, until the cake is golden brown, pulling away from the sides of the pan, and the top springs back slightly when pressed. A cake tester or toothpick inserted in the center should come out clean.

Remove the cake from the oven and let cool for 5–10 minutes. The cake should still be very warm, but cool enough to handle. Remove the cake from the pan and place pan-side down on a wire rack or cutting board. Slice the domed top off the cake and discard or save for another use.

Remove the ice cream bowl from freezer and peel back the top layer of plastic wrap. Gently flip the cake upside down, placing the still-warm, cut side of the cake down on top of the ice cream. It should fit snugly inside the rim of the bowl. Gently press the cake down to ensure it makes full contact with the ice cream. Cover again with plastic wrap and return to the freezer for at least 6 hours, up to overnight.

Remove the ice cream bowl from freezer. Fill a slightly larger bowl about ⅓ of the way with hot water. Carefully lower the ice cream bowl into the hot water, ensuring that the water line is well below the rim of the bowl so it doesn't spill over.

Set a wire rack inside a baking sheet. Peel back the plastic wrap and carefully invert the ice cream bowl onto the center of the wire rack. Remove the bowl and plastic wrap.

Using the hot water in the larger bowl, warm an offset spatula for a few seconds. Use the spatula to smooth out any creases in the ice cream left by the plastic wrap. The surface of the ice cream should be as smooth as possible. If there are any gaps between the ice cream and cake, fill in with the leftover ice cream. If the ice cream has started to melt at all, return to the freezer until completely frozen again, 1–2 hours.

Make the chocolate glaze: Add the chocolate, butter, and corn syrup to a medium microwave-safe bowl. Microwave in 30-second intervals, whisking between, until completely melted. Whisk vigorously until glaze is smooth and glossy. Let cool to about 100°F (38°C), or just warm to the touch, before using.

Pour the chocolate glaze directly over the top of the ice cream dome in one continuous pour, using a spatula to ensure the chocolate leaves the bowl quickly. Ensure the bombe is covered completely by swirling the chocolate in a 2-inch circle over the top center of the dome.

Let the bombe sit at room temperature 5–10 minutes for the ice cream to soften slightly and the glaze to set, or place in the refrigerator for up to 30 minutes. If serving more than 30 minutes later, return to the freezer, then let the bombe thaw at room temperature for 15–20 minutes before slicing and serving.

Enjoy!

Avocado Strawberry Ice Cream

Ingredients

for 4 servings

- 16 oz heavy whipping cream(170 g)

- 14 oz condensed milk(395 g)

- 1 cup strawberry(150 g)

- ¼ cup powdered sugar(25 g)

- 3 avocados

Preparation

1. Whisk heavy whipping cream until you reach soft peaks.

2. Blend the strawberries, avocados and condensed milk.

3. Mix everything into the whipped cream and add powdered sugar.

4. Place the mix into the avocado shells and add a thin slice of strawberry on top.

5. As an option, put leftovers in a bowl with slices of strawberry.

6. Freeze for two hours.

7. Enjoy!

Peach Cobbler

Ingredients

for 8 servings

PEACH FILLING

- 10 medium peaches

- 1 ¼ cups dark brown sugar (250 g)

- ½ teaspoon cinnamon

- ¼ teaspoon ground nutmeg

- 1 tablespoon vanilla extract

- 1 teaspoon lemon juice

- ½ teaspoon kosher salt

- ⅛ teaspoon black pepper

- 1 ½ tablespoons cornstarch

- ½ stick unsalted butter, cubed

CRUST

- 4 tablespoons unsalted butter, melted, plus more for greasing

- ¼ cup all purpose flour(55 g), plus more for dusting

- 3 refrigerated pie crusts, 9 in (22 cm)

- 1 large egg yolk

- 1 tablespoon water

- 2 tablespoons granulated sugar

- ½ teaspoon cinnamon

- vanilla ice cream, for serving

Preparation

1. Preheat the oven to 425°F (220°C).

2. Peel, pit, and slice the peaches into wedges. You should have about 10 cups.

3. Make the peach filling: In a large pot, combine the brown sugar, cinnamon, nutmeg, vanilla, lemon juice, salt, pepper, and peaches. Turn the heat to medium and gently stir until the sugar is completely dissolved. Cook for 3–5 minutes, until the mixture is simmering and the peaches have started to release their juices.

4. In a small bowl, mix the cornstarch with 2 tablespoons of syrup from the pot until the cornstarch dissolves. Stir the mixture back into the filling and

bring to boil. Cook until the syrup thickens and turns opaque, 3–4 minutes. Remove the pot from the heat.

5. Make the crust: Grease a 9 x 13-inch casserole dish with melted butter.

6. On a lightly floured flat surface, unroll 2 of the pie crusts. Overlap the crusts at the center so it looks like a Venn diagram, then use a floured rolling pin to roll over the overlapping portions to seal together. Flour the top of the crust, then roll onto the rolling pin. Unroll over the prepared baking dish. Gently lift the edges of the crust so the bottom sits flush against the bottom of the baking dish. Let the edges hang over the sides of the pan.

7. Use a slotted spoon to transfer the peach filling into the crust, draining off any excess juices. Save any leftover syrup for serving. Dollop the cubed butter over the peaches.

8. Lightly roll out the remaining pie crust, then unroll over the peach filling. Fold the edges of the top and bottom crusts together to seal.

9. In a small bowl, whisk the egg yolk with the water. Brush all over the top of the crust.

10. In a separate small bowl, mix together the sugar and cinnamon. Liberally sprinkle over the crust.

11. Cut 3 large diagonal slits into the top of the crust to release steam.

12. Bake the cobbler for 35–45 minutes, until the crust is golden brown and the filling is bubbling. If the edges of the crust are getting too dark, cover with foil and continue baking.

13. Let the cobbler cool for 25–30 minutes before serving with vanilla ice cream. Drizzle with some of the reserved peach syrup.

14. Enjoy!

Vegan Spotted Dick & Custard

Ingredients

for 6 servings

- ½ lb self raising flour(225 g)

- ½ teaspoon baking powder

- 1 cup vegan butter(125 g), frozen then grated

- ¼ cup caster sugar(75 g)

- 1 cup currants(120 g)

- ½ orange, zest

- ½ lemon, zest

- ½ cup coconut milk(190 mL)

- vegan butter, for greasing

CUSTARD

- 2 ½ tablespoons corn flour

- ⅛ teaspoon turmeric

- 4 tablespoons water

- ½ cup caster sugar(100 g)

- 2 cups coconut milk(400 mL)

- ½ cup vegan double cream(150 mL)

- 2 tablespoons vanilla extract

Preparation

1. In a large bowl add the flour, baking powder and vegan butter. Using the tips of your fingers rub together until it resembles breadcrumbs.

2. Next add the sugar, currants, zest of an orange and lemon. Stir until fully combined.

3. Make a well in the centre of the dry ingredients and add the coconut milk. Stir until a wet dough forms.

4. Place the dough into a greased pudding basin. Place greaseproof paper over the top of the dough and cover with a lid. If your basin doesn't have a lid simply use tin foil.

5. Take a large pot and place a small up-turned saucer into the bottom. Next take a large piece of greaseproof paper and fold into a long strip and place it into the pot. (You want it to be long enough so it sits along the bottom and up the sides of the basin)

6. Place the basin on top of the saucer and grease proof paper. Fill the pot ¼ full of cold water, cover with a lid and place over a low-medium heat.

7. Once the water comes to a simmer cook the pudding for around 1 hour 30 minutes or until the sponge is cooked through.

8. To a small bowl add the cornflour, turmeric & water. Stir until combined and set aside.

9. Next add the caster sugar, vanilla extract, coconut milk & vegan double cream. Whisk until combined and then pour in your cornflour mix. Stir until fully combined.

10. Place a medium sized pan over a medium heat and your custard mix. Cook for 10 minutes (or until it has thickened and glossy) continuously stirring.

11. Once cooked, remove from heat and enjoy!

Snow White Poison Candy Apples

Ingredients

for 4 servings

- 4 honeycrisp apples, stems removed

- 1 ½ cups sugar(300 g)

- ½ cup water(120 mL)

- ¼ cup light corn syrup(85 g)

- 6 drops red food coloring

- 8 oz neon green candy melts(225 g)

- 1 teaspoon canola oil

SPECIAL EQUIPMENT

- 4 lollipop sticks

Preparation

1. Insert a lollipop stick into the stem end of each apple.

2. Line a baking sheet with parchment paper or wax paper.

3. Add the sugar, water, and corn syrup to a medium saucepan fitted with a candy thermometer. Bring to a boil over medium heat, then cook until the temperature reaches 300°F (150°C), about 5 minutes. Remove the pot from the heat and stir in the red food coloring.

4. Dip the apples in the syrup to coat entirely, then set on the prepared baking sheet. Let cool until the candy hardens, about 5 minutes.

5. Add the green candy melts to a medium microwave-safe bowl. Microwave on low power in 20-second intervals, stirring between, until melted. Stir in the canola oil until smooth. Let cool slightly, then transfer to a squeeze bottle. Let cool for 5 minutes more, or until the candy sets quickly when squeezed out of the bottle.

6. Use the melted candy to draw eyes and a mouth on each apple, then outline the rest of the apple above the very bottom and fill in the space outside the eyes and mouth.

7. Let set for 10–15 minutes, until completely hardened.

8. Enjoy!

6-Hour Salted Caramel Deep Dish Apple Pie

Ingredients

for 8 servings

PIE DOUGH

- 3 ¾ cups all purpose flour(465 g), plus more for dusting

- 1 pinch kosher salt

- 3 sticks unsalted butter, cut into 1/2 in (1.24 cm) and frozen for 15 minutes

- ¾ cup water(180 mL), ice water, plus more as needed

- 1 large egg, with 1 tablespoon water

FILLING

- 2 tablespoons unsalted butter

- 3 lb Granny Smith applesGranny Smith apples(1.2 g), peeled and sliced into ¼-inch (6 mm) wedges

- 3 lb honeycrisp apple(1.2 g), peeled and sliced into ¼-inch (6 mm) wedges

- 1 lemon

- 1 ½ cups brown sugar(300 g)

- 1 teaspoon kosher salt

- 1 tablespoon pumpkin pie spice

- 1 ½ teaspoons vanilla bean paste

- ¼ cup cornstarch(30 g)

- 3 tablespoons water

APPLE CIDER SYRUP

- 1 cup apple cider(240 mL)

SALTED CARAMEL

- 1 ½ cups granulated sugar(300 g)

- ⅓ cup water(180 mL)

- 1 tablespoon light corn syrup

- ¾ cup heavy cream(180 mL), room temperature

- ½ teaspoon kosher salt

- pecan, candied chopped, for garnish

Preparation

1. Make the pie dough: In a large bowl, mix together the flour and salt. Add the butter and toss to coat each cube with the flour, then smash each piece of butter with your fingers.

2. Add the ice water, 1–2 tablespoons at a time, and continue to toss until the dough holds together when pressed between your hands. You may not need all of the water, but if the dough is too dry, add more, 1 teaspoon at a time, as needed. The dough should not be very tacky or sticky.

3. Turn the dough onto a clean surface. Work into 2 discs and cover with plastic wrap. Refrigerate for at least 1 hour.

4. Make the filling: Melt the butter in a large Dutch oven over medium heat. Add the apples, lemon juice, brown sugar, salt, pumpkin pie spice, and vanilla bean paste. Stir to coat the apples well and cook until they start to soften and release their juices and the sugar dissolves, 5–7 minutes.

5. In a small bowl, whisk together the cornstarch and water. Pour the slurry over the apples, increase the heat to high, and cook until the juices are boiling and thickened, 3–4 minutes.

6. Remove the pot from the heat and let the filling cool to room temperature, about 30 minutes.

7. Make the apple cider syrup: Add the apple cider to a small saucepan over medium heat. Bring to boil and cook until reduced to 2 tablespoons with the consistency of maple syrup, about 10 minutes. Remove the pot from the heat and let the syrup cool to room temperature.

8. Assemble the pie: On a floured surface, roll a disc of pie dough into a 12-inch (30 cm) round, about ¼ inch (6 mm) thick. Transfer to a 9-inch (22 cm) deep dish pie plate.

9. Add the apple filling to the crust, along with any accumulated juices from the bottom of the bowl. Drizzle the apple cider syrup on top. Refrigerate while you roll out the other dough.

10. Roll out the remaining dough disc to a 12-inch (30 cm) round. Drape over the pie, then pinch the edges together. Trim any excess dough around the edges, then roll the edges under all the way around the pie. Use the knuckle of an index finger on one hand and your index finger and thumb on the other hand to make large crimps around the edges.

11. Brush the dough all over with the egg wash. Use a paring knife to cut a few vents in the top to allow steam to escape.

12. Transfer the assembled pie to the freezer for 20 minutes, until firm.

13. Preheat the oven to 350°F (200°C). Line a baking sheet with aluminum foil.

14. Place the pie dish on the prepared baking sheet, then transfer to the oven and bake for 80–90 minutes, covering with foil halfway through. Cook until the juices are bubbling and the crust is golden brown. Remove the pie from the oven and let cool for at least 1 hour.

15. Meanwhile, make the salted caramel: Add the sugar, water, and corn syrup to a large saucepan over medium-high heat. Bring to a low boil and cook until the sugar dissolves and mixture starts to turn a light copper color, about 10 minutes.

16. Remove the pot from the heat and stir in the cream and salt until incorporated. If the caramel seems too thin, return to medium low heat and boil until thickened to your desired consistency, 1–2 minutes. Transfer the caramel to a heat-proof liquid measuring cup and let cool to room temperature, 30–60 minutes.

17. Pour the cooled caramel sauce over the pie and garnish with candied pecans.

18. Slice and serve.

19. Enjoy!

Sweet Corn And Blueberry Swirl Ice Cream

Ingredients

for 8 servings

- 2 ears corn, shucked
- 2 cups heavy cream(480 mL), divided
- ¼ teaspoon kosher salt
- 1 cup blueberry(100 g)
- ¼ cup granulated sugar(50 g)
- 1 teaspoon lemon juice
- 14 oz condensed milk(395 g), 1 can, chilled

Preparation

1. Remove the corn kernels from the cob with a knife. Then, carefully break the cobs in half with your hands.

2. Place the corn kernels in a food processor. Pulse several times until coarsely chopped.

3. Add the chopped kernels, cobs, 1½ cups (360 ml) of cream, and the salt to a large saucepan. Stir to ensure the ingredients are well combined. Cover and cook over low heat for 20 minutes.

4. Remove the cream and corn mixture from the heat and chill in the refrigerator for at least 2 hours.

5. Combine the blueberries, sugar, and lemon juice in a medium bowl. Let sit at room temperature for 10 minutes, or until the berries appear juicy and vibrant, stirring occasionally.

6. Transfer the berry mixture to a food processor or blender and puree. Set aside.

7. Remove the corn cobs from the chilled cream mixture. Pour the remaining corn cream through a sieve into a large bowl. Use the back of a spoon or spatula to press the solids to extract any remaining liquid.

8. Add the remaining heavy cream. Using an electric hand mixer, whip the cream mixture until soft peaks form. Fold in the condensed milk with a rubber spatula.

9. Pour half of the cream mixture into a 9x5-inch (23x13-cm) loaf pan. Top with half of the blueberry puree and use a knife to swirl it into the cream.

10. Top with the remaining cream and puree, then swirl the puree with a knife again.

11. Freeze for 3-4 hours before serving. If the ice cream is too solid to scoop, let sit at room temperature for 10-15 minutes before scooping.

12. Enjoy!

Magic Fizzy Truffles

Ingredients

for 4 servings

- nonstick cooking spray

- 2 teaspoons baking soda

- 1 packet strawberry drink mix

- 1 cup sugar(200 g)

- 3 tablespoons light corn starch syrup

- ½ cup heavy cream(120 mL)

- 10 oz chocolate chips(285 g), bittersweet

Preparation

1. Spray some non-stick cooking spray to a cooking parchment sheet. In a bowl, add the strawberry drink mix and baking soda and set aside. Add light corn starch syrup and sugar to a heated pan and mix thoroughly. Let it heat at 275 degrees F for 5 minutes. Add to the pan, the bowl mix(prepared beforehand) and after whisking thoroughly, transfer the entire mix to the parchment paper. Let it cool for 20 minutes.

2. In a clean pan, add heavy cream and let simmer. Transfer the cream into a bowl of chocolate chips and let it sit for 5 minutes. After thoroughly mixing the cream and chocolate chips, refrigerate for about 45-60 minutes.

3. Crumble the strawberry mix and set aside half. Add the other half to a blender and blend till the consistency is power-like.

4. Add single chunks of the strawberry filling to single scoops of chocolate balls. Repeat about 12 times. Finally, cover the chocolate ball with the strawberry powder.

5. Enjoy!

2-Hour Strawberry Cheesecake

Ingredients

for 8 servings

GRAHAM CRACKER CRUST

- 1 ½ cups graham cracker crumbs(170 g)

- ¼ cup sugar(50 g)

- 1 stick unsalted butter, melted

FILLING

- 8 oz cream cheese(225 g), room temperature

- 6 oz sour cream(170 g), room temprature

- ¾ cup sugar(150 g)

- 3 medium eggs, room temperature

- 1 tablespoon vanilla extract, or vanilla bean paste

STRAWBERRY TOPPING

- 1 lb strawberry(455 g), stemmed and haled

- ¾ cup sugar(150 g)

- 2 tablespoons corn syrup

- 3 tablespoons water

- 2 tablespoons cornstarch

Preparation

1. Make the crust: Preheat the oven to 350°F (180°C).

2. Add the graham cracker crumbs, sugar, and melted butter to a medium bowl and mix well.

3. Transfer the crumbs to a 9-inch pie dish and press evenly against the bottom and up the sides.

4. Bake the crust for 5–10 minutes, until firm.

5. Remove the crust from the oven and let cool. Reduce the oven temperature to 300°F (150°C).

6. Make the filling: In the bowl of a stand mixer fitted with the paddle attachment, combine the cream cheese and beat until smooth. Add the sour cream and beat on medium speed until well incorporated, scraping down the sides of the bowl as neede. Add the sugar and beat to combine. Add the eggs, 1 at a time, beating until well combined before adding the next addition. Add the vanilla and beat to incorporate.

7. Pour the cream cheese filling into the prepared crust.

8. Bake for 45–60 minutes, until mostly set but still slightly jiggly at the center. The cheesecake will continue to set as it cools.

9. Remove the cheesecake from the oven and chill in the refrigerator for 1 hour, or until set.

10. Make the strawberry topping: Add the strawberries, sugar, and corn syrup to a medium skillet over medium-high heat. Cook until syrupy, but the strawberry halves are mostly intact, about 5 minutes.

11. In a small bowl, whisk together the water and cornstarch. Add to the strawberry mixture and cook until thick and glossy, 2–3 minutes. Transfer the topping to a heatproof bowl and refrigerate until cool.

12. When ready to serve, pour the topping over the cheesecake and spread evenly. Slice and serve.

13. Enjoy!

SNACK RECIPES FOR BIPOLAR DISORDER

Pretzel Bites With Mustard Cheese Sauce

Ingredients

for 8 servings

- 1 ½ lb pizza dough(680 g)

- ¼ cup baking soda(45 g)

- 1 egg, whisked

- coarse salt

- ¼ cup butter(55 g)

- ¼ cup flour(30 g)

- 2 cups milk(480 mL)

- 1 ½ tablespoons French's Honey Mustard

- 2 cups shredded cheddar cheese(200 g)

- 2 teaspoons apple cider vinegar

- 1 ½ teaspoons salt

- 1 teaspoon pepper

Preparation

1. Preheat oven to 425°F (218 C)

2. Roll pizza dough into balls slightly smaller than the size of a golf ball.

3. Bring a pot of water to a simmer, then stir in the baking soda. Add dough balls and cook for 30 seconds. Remove from the water and place them on a parchment-lined sheet tray.

4. Brush each dough ball with egg wash and sprinkle with a bit of coarse salt. Place tray in oven and bake for 10–12 minutes, until pretzels turn a deep brown color.

5. Melt the butter in a saucepan over low heat. Whisk in the flour and cook for 1 minute. Pour in the milk while whisking. Cook for 2–3 minutes, stirring occasionally, until the milk begins to thicken slightly. Add in the French's Honey Mustard, cheese, apple cider vinegar, salt, and pepper. Whisk until cheese melts and the sauce is smooth. Let the cheese sauce bubble for a few

more minutes to thicken up slightly. Serve immediately with the pretzel bites!

6. Enjoy!

Bacon Jam Hacks

Ingredients

for 2 cups

- 1 lb bacon(455 g), thick-cut, cut into 1in (2 1/2 cm) pieces

- 1 large yellow onion, finely chopped

- 4 cloves garlic, minced

- ⅓ cup apple cider vinegar(80 mL)

- ½ cup dark brown sugar(110 g), packed

- ½ cup maple syrup(168 g)

- ½ teaspoon cayenne

- ½ teaspoon ground cumin

- 2 teaspoons kosher salt

- 1 ½ teaspoons black pepper

Preparation

1. Add the bacon to a cold large skillet. Turn the heat to medium and cook the bacon until crispy, 18–22 minutes. Using a slotted spoon, transfer the cooked bacon to a paper towel-lined plate to drain, leaving the rendered bacon grease in the pan.

2. Reduce the heat to low. Add the onion and garlic to the pan with the bacon fat. Slowly cook the onions and garlic, stirring occasionally, until completely softened and dark golden brown, 70–80 minutes.

3. Add the apple cider vinegar to the pan and cook, stirring frequently, until the liquid is reduced by half, about 10 minutes. Add the brown sugar, maple syrup, cayenne, cumin, salt, pepper and stir to incorporate. Return the cooked bacon to the pan. Continue to stir until a jam-like consistency is reached, another 5 minutes.

4. Let cool for 5–10 minutes, then transfer the mixture to a food processor and pulse until mostly smooth with a bit of texture, similar to pesto. Transfer to a glass bowl to cool completely, skimming any excess fat that rises to the top.

5. Store the jam in an airtight container in the refrigerator for up to 4 weeks. Warm before serving, then use on toast, mac 'n' cheese, and more!

6. Enjoy!

Mini Strudels 4 Ways

Ingredients

for 8 servings

STRUDELS

- 2 sheets frozen puff pastry, thawed

- 1 large egg, beaten

BLUEBERRY PEACH FILLING

- 2 tablespoons peach jam

- 2 tablespoons blueberry

CRANBERRY ORANGE FILLING

- 2 tablespoons orange marmalade

- 2 tablespoons fresh cranberries

HAM AND SWISS FILLING

- 2 slices swiss cheese, quartered

- 2 slices ham, quartered

- ½ teaspoon freshly ground black pepper

PROSCIUTTO AND ASPARAGUS FILLING

- 4 slices prosciutto

- 10 pieces asparagus, cut into 2 in pieces (5 cm)

- ½ teaspoon freshly ground black pepper

Preparation

1. Preheat the oven to 400°F (200°C). Line a baking sheet with parchment paper.

2. Cut the puff pastry sheets into 2 x 5-inch (5 cm x 12 cm) rectangles. You should have 16 rectangles total.

3. Make the blueberry peach strudels: In a small bowl, mix together the peach jam and blueberries. Scoop 1 tablespoon of the mixture onto the bottom third of 4 pastry rectangles. Brush the exposed pastry with the beaten egg, then fold the bottom of the pastry over the filling and continue rolling to seal. Place seam-side down on the prepared baking sheet. Cut 2 diagonal slits on the top of each strudel and brush with more egg wash.

4. Make the cranberry orange strudels: In a small bowl, mix together the orange marmalade and cranberries. Scoop 1 tablespoon of the mixture onto the bottom third of 4 pastry rectangles. Brush the exposed pastry with the beaten egg, then fold the bottom of the pastry over the filling and continue rolling to seal. Place seam-side down on the prepared baking sheet. Cut 2 diagonal slits on the top of each strudel and brush with more egg wash.

5. Make the ham and Swiss strudels: Place 2 Swiss cheese quarters and 2 ham quarters at the bottom third of 4 pastry rectangles. Brush the exposed pastry with the beaten egg, then fold the bottom of the pastry over the filling and continue rolling to seal. Place seam-side down on the prepared baking sheet. Cut 2 diagonal slits on the top of each strudel. Brush with more egg wash and top with a pinch of pepper.

6. Make the prosciutto asparagus strudels: Wrap a slice of prosciutto around 2 or 3 pieces of asparagus and place at the bottom third of 4 pastry rectangles. Brush the exposed pastry with the beaten egg, then fold the bottom of the pastry over the filling and continue rolling to seal. Place seam-side down on the prepared baking sheet. Cut 2 diagonal slits on the top of each strudel. Brush with more egg wash and top with a pinch of pepper.

7. Bake the strudels for 30 minutes, until puffed and golden brown.

8. Enjoy!

Fresh Seacuterie Board

Ingredients

for 6 servings

OCTOPUS SALAD

- 1 teaspoon orange zest

- 2 tablespoons fresh orange juice

- 1 teaspoon ginger juice

- 1 small clove garlic, grated

- 2 tablespoons low sodium soy sauce

- 1 ½ teaspoons toasted sesame oil

- 2 tablespoons unsweetened mirin

- 1 tablespoon apple cider vinegar

- 1 fresno chilie, seeded and minced

- ½ teaspoon sugar

- 1 tablespoon olive oil, plus 1½ teaspoons

- 1 ¼ teaspoons kosher salt

- ¾ lb frozen cooked octopus(340 g), thawed, cut into ¼-inch (6 mm) rounds

- micro cilantro, for serving

MIGNONETTE SAUCE

- 1 small shallot, minced

- ½ cup red wine vinegar(120 mL)

- ½ teaspoon crushed black peppercorns

CRAB DIP

- 2 tablespoons cream cheese

- 1 tablespoon mayonnaise

- 2 teaspoons old bay seasoning

- ⅛ teaspoon garlic powder

- 1 ½ teaspoons prepared horseradish

- 1 teaspoon lemon zest

- 1 tablespoon lemon juice

- 3 dashes worcestershire sauce

- ½ lb fresh crab meat(225 g)

- 2 tablespoons fresh chives, plus more for garnish

- 1 ¼ teaspoons kosher salt

OYSTERS

- 8 fresh oysters

ASSEMBLY

- 6 cups crushed ice(840 g), plus more as needed

- 2 butter lettuce leaves

- ½ lb prepared ahi poke salad(225 g)

- 1 lb lox(455 g)

- 1 lb cocktail shrimp(455 g), tails on

- ½ cup cocktail sauce(160 g)

- 2 tablespoons prepared horseradish

- ½ cup seaweed salad(70 g)

- 4 slices grilled bread

- 8 crackers, of choice

- 1 english cucumber, sliced on the diagonal into 1/4 in (6mm) rounds

- ½ lb crab claws(225 g)

- 1 blood orange, sliced

- 1 cup pickled vegetable(150 g), such as peppadews and onion

- 1 tablespoon caper, drained

- decoratively cut lemon

SPECIAL EQUIPMENT

- oyster knife

- 2 baking sheets, 26 x 18-inch (66 x 45 cm)

- brown butchers paper

Preparation

1. The day before serving, make the octopus salad: In a large bowl, whisk together the orange zest, orange juice, ginger juice, garlic, soy sauce, sesame oil, mirin, apple cider vinegar, jalapeño, sugar, olive oil, and salt. Add the octopus and toss to coat. Cover the bowl with plastic wrap and marinate the octopus in the refrigerator overnight.

2. Make the mignonette sauce: In a small serving bowl, stir together the shallot, red wine vinegar, and crushed black peppercorns. Refrigerate until ready to serve.

3. Make the crab dip. In a medium bowl, stir together the cream cheese, mayonnaise, Old Bay seasoning, garlic powder, horseradish, lemon zest and juice, Worcestershire sauce, and salt. Mix well. Gently fold in the crab meat and chives, then season with the salt. Refrigerate until ready to serve.

4. Shuck the oysters: Wrap a kitchen towel around your hand and an oyster, leaving the pointed end of the oyster exposed. Using an oyster knife, carefully wedge the knife into one side of the point and use firm, even pressure to twist to open the oyster. Unwrap the oyster from the towel, then use the knife to work around the top shell, disconnecting the muscle. Remove the top shell and gently run the knife along the bottom shell to release the oyster. Repeat with the remaining oysters. Arrange the oysters in the bottom shells on a small platter of crushed ice with the mignonette sauce and a lemon half.

5. Assemble the board: Spread the crushed ice on a 26 x 18-inch baking sheet. Top with the other baking sheet. Line with butcher's paper.

6. Transfer the octopus salad to a serving dish and garnish with the micro cilantro, then place on the pan, along with the oyster platter. Transfer the crab dip to a serving dish and place on the pan, then garnish with chives. Add the butter lettuce leaves, then top with the ahi poke salad. Arrange the lox, cocktail shrimp, cocktail sauce, prepared horseradish, seaweed salad, grilled bread, crackers, cucumber, crab claws, blood orange slices, and pickled vegetables. Top the lox with the capers. Add the lemons to the pan.

7. Serve immediately.

8. Enjoy!

Sweet & Spicy Peach Sticky Wings

Ingredients

for 4 servings

BBQ DRY RUB

- 1 ½ teaspoons chipotle powder
- 1 ½ teaspoons smoked paprika
- 1 ½ teaspoons baking powder
- 1 ½ teaspoons onion powder
- 1 ½ teaspoons garlic powder
- 1 ½ teaspoons kosher salt
- ½ teaspoon cayenne
- ½ teaspoon italian seasoning
- ½ teaspoon cumin
- ¼ teaspoon black pepper

WINGS

- 2 lb chicken wings (900 g)
- 2 tablespoons canola oil
- fresh cilantro, chopped, for garnish

PEACH GLAZE

- 1 can peaches, in heavy syrup
- ¼ cup dark brown sugar (50 g)
- 1 tablespoon apple cider vinegar
- 1 tablespoon soy sauce
- 1 tablespoon sriracha
- 1 ½ teaspoons cinnamon
- ¼ teaspoon black pepper
- ¼ teaspoon kosher salt
- 1 bay leaf, dried

- ¾ cup water (180 mL)

- 1 tablespoon cold unsalted butter

Preparation

1. Preheat the oven to 425°F (220°C). Line a large baking sheet with foil and grease with nonstick spray.

2. Make the dry rub: Add the chipotle powder, paprika, baking powder, onion powder, garlic powder, salt, cayenne, Italian seasoning, cumin, and black pepper to a bowl and whisk until evenly combined.

3. Make the wings: Add the chicken wings to a large bowl and toss with the oil. Sprinkle in the dry rub and use your hands to massage it into the chicken wings.

4. Arrange the wings on the prepared baking sheet, spacing evenly. Bake for 15 minutes, then flip and continue baking for another 15 minutes.

5. While the chicken wings are baking, make the glaze: Add the peaches in syrup, brown sugar, apple cider vinegar, soy sauce, Sriracha, cinnamon, black pepper, salt, bay leaf, and water to a medium pan. Stir to combine, then bring to a boil over medium-high heat, then reduce the heat to medium and cook for 15 minutes, until the peaches have softened and sauce has thickened.

6. Remove the bay leaf, then transfer the peach mixture to a blender and purée on high speed for 30–60 seconds. Strain the glaze through a fine-mesh strainer back into the pan. Turn the heat to high and cook until the glaze has thickened, about 5 minutes. Whisk in the butter until fully incorporated. The glaze should coat the back of a spoon.

7. Carefully remove the wings from the oven and brush on both sides with about ⅓ of the glaze. Return to the oven and cook for another 5 minutes.

8. Remove wings from the oven brush with another ⅓ of the glaze. Turn the oven to high broil, return the wings to the oven, and broil for 2–3 minutes, or until the glaze is bubbling.

9. Remove from the oven and toss wings in a large bowl with the remaining glaze.

10. Transfer to a serving plate and garnish with the cilantro.

11. Enjoy!

Green Goddess CBD Dip

Ingredients

for 2 cups

- 1 cup watercress(40 g), or spanish

- 2 scallions, white and light green parts only, roughly chopped

- ¼ cup fresh mint leaf(10 g)

- ¼ cup fresh chives(10 g), chopped

- ¼ cup fresh dill(10 g), packed

- ¼ cup fresh parsley(10 g), packed

- ¼ cup fresh basil(10 g), packed

- 1 tablespoon fresh tarragon

- 1 clove garlic, minced

- 1 ½ teaspoons lemon zest

- 1 tablespoon lemon juice

- ½ cup mayonnaise(120 g)

- ¼ cup sour cream(60 g)

- 1 teaspoon CBD oil, optional

- ¼ teaspoon anchovy paste

- 1 teaspoon kosher salt

FOR SERVING

- watermelon radish, shaved

- persian cucumber, sliced

- carrot, halved

- snap pea

- cauliflower

- mini bell pepper, sliced

- broccoli floret

- celery stick

- quartered radish

- ¼ lemon, cut into wedges

Preparation

1. In a food processor, combine the watercress, scallions, mint, chives, dill, parsley, basil, and tarragon. Process until all herbs are finely chopped, about 30 seconds. Scrape down the sides of the bowl with a small spatula and pulse a few more times. Add the garlic, lemon zest, lemon juice, mayonnaise, crème fraîche, CBD oil, if using, anchovy paste, and salt. Process until smooth but the herbs are still intact, about 15 seconds. Scrape down the sides of the bowl again and pulse a few more times.

2. Transfer the dip to a serving bowl and set in the center of a large platter.

3. Arrange the vegetables around the dip then squeeze the lemon wedges over the vegetables.

4. Enjoy!

Cucumber Celery Juice

Ingredients

for 2 servings

- 8 large celery stalks, rinsed and roughly chopped

- 1 large cucumber, roughly chopped

- 1 granny smith apple, cored and roughly chopped

- 1 cup Pure Leaf® Green Tea(240 mL)

- 1 large lemon, juiced

- 2 lemon wheels

- 2 cucumber wheels

- ice, for serving

Preparation

1. Add the celery, cucumber, apple, and Pure Leaf® Green Tea to a blender and blend on high speed until smooth, 3–4 minutes.

2. Strain the juice through a fine-mesh sieve set over a large bowl, using a spatula to press the pulp to extract all of the liquid. Discard the pulp. Stir in the lemon juice.

3. Fill 2 glasses with ice, then divide the juice evenly between the glasses and garnish each with a lemon wheel and a cucumber wheel.

4. Enjoy!

Banana Pepper Poppers

Ingredients

for 2 servings

- 10 banana peppers, halved lengthwise and deseeded
- 2 tablespoons cream cheese
- 2 cloves garlic, minced
- 1 tablespoon cheese
- 1 teaspoon freshly ground cumin powder
- 1 tablespoon panko
- chive
- fresh parsley
- salt and pepper

Preparation

1. Mix all the ingredients together (other than the chives and parsley).

2. Spoon the mixture into the peppers and drizzle with olive oil.

3. Bake for 15 minutes at 425°F until they are golden brown and the peppers are tender.

4. Serve warm.

Back-To-School Snack Board

Ingredients

for 8 servings

FRUIT KEBABS

- 1 small pineapple, peeled, cored, and diced

- 3 Mandarin orange slices, peeled and segments separated

- 3 large kiwis, peeled and cut into half moons

- 1 bunch red seedless grapes

PINWHEELS

- 4 spinach tortillas
- 8 teaspoons honey mustard
- 8 slices roasted turkey
- 12 slices american cheese
- 16 green leaf lettuces

AB & J SANDWICHES

- 8 slices white bread
- 4 tablespoons almond butter
- 4 tablespoons strawberry preserve

PIMIENTO CHEESE DIP

- 1 block cheddar cheese, room temperature
- 1 jar pimiento peppers, drained
- ¼ cup cream cheese(55 g), softened
- ¼ cup mayonnaise(60 g)

- 2 dashes hot sauce, optional

CUCUMBER HUMMUS BOATS

- 4 persian cucumbers

- ½ cup hummus(120 g)

- ¼ teaspoon sweet paprika

FOR ASSEMBLY

- trail mix

- Fish-shaped cheese cracker

- Pretzel twist

- kettle corn

- butter cracker

SPECIAL EQUIPMENT

- 12 wooden skewers

- round cutter

- 18-inch board

Preparation

1. Make the fruit kebabs: Thread the pineapple, orange segments, kiwi, and grapes onto 12 6-inch skewers, alternating between fruits. Store the kebabs in an airtight container or zip-top bag in the refrigerator until ready to serve, up to 2 days.

2. Make the pinwheels: Spread 2 teaspoons of honey mustard evenly over each tortilla, then layer 2 slices of turkey, 3 slices of American cheese, and 4 lettuce leaves on top. Fold in the sides of each tortilla, then roll into a tight log. Wrap the logs in plastic wrap and store in the refrigerator until ready to serve, up to 3 days. Just before serving, slice each log crosswise into 8 pinwheels.

3. Make the AB & J sandwiches: Spread 1 tablespoon of almond butter on the centers of 4 slices of bread. Spread 1 tablespoon of preserves on the centers of the remaining 4 slices of bread. Sandwich the almond butter and preserves slices together. Using a 4-inch round cutter, press firmly to cut out the centers of each sandwich and discard the crusts. Using a 4-inch sandwich crimper, press down firmly to seal the edges of the sandwich together. Alternatively, using your fingers, press the edges of the sandwiches together to seal, then use a fork to crimp the edges. Store the sandwiches in an airtight container or zip-top bag in the refrigerator until ready to serve, up to 2 days.

4. Make the pimiento cheese dip: Finely grate the cheddar cheese on the small holes of a box grater, then transfer to a large bowl. Add the pimientos, cream cheese, mayonnaise, and hot sauce, if using, and stir with a rubber spatula until well incorporated and creamy. Store the dip in an airtight container in the refrigerator until ready to serve, up to 5 days. Transfer to a serving bowl before assembling the board.

5. Make the cucumber hummus boats: Cut the cucumbers in half lengthwise. Using a spoon, scoop the seeds out of each half. Fill each cucumber boat with 1 tablespoon of hummus, smoothing with the back of a spoon. Sprinkle with paprika.

6. When ready to assemble, add the pimiento cheese dip, trail mix, and fish-shaped cheese crackers to small serving bowls. Place on a large board or platter, then surround with the fruit kebabs, AB & J sandwiches, pinwheels, cucumber boats, pretzels, kettle corn, and butter crackers.

7. Enjoy!

Lumpia (Lumpiang Shanghai)

Ingredients

for 50 Lumpias

- 2 small carrots, peeled and cut into 1-inch (2.54 cm) pieces

- 1 small sweet onion, quartered

- 1 water chestnut

- 1 lb ground pork (425 g)

- 3 green onions, thinly sliced

- 6 cloves garlic, minced

- 2 tablespoons soy sauce

- 1 tablespoon Maggi seasoning

- 1 teaspoon sugar

- 1 ½ teaspoons freshly ground black pepper

- 1 large egg, lightly beaten

- 1 package Filipino lumpia wrappers, thawed (preferably Pamana or Tropics brand)

- 2 tablespoons all purpose flour

- 2 tablespoons water

- canola oil, for frying

- Banana ketchup, sweet chili sauce, or sweet and sour sauce, for serving

Preparation

1. Add the carrots, onion, and water chestnuts to the bowl of a food processor. Pulse until the vegetables are finely chopped, but not ground into a paste.

2. Transfer the vegetables to a large bowl with the ground pork, green onions, garlic, soy sauce, Knorr seasoning, sugar, black pepper, and egg. Stir with a fork until well combined; do not overmix. Cover the bowl with plastic wrap and refrigerate for 1 hour.

3. Gently separate the lumpia wrappers from one another and cover with a damp towel to prevent them from drying out.

4. Add the flour and water to a small bowl and whisk to combine, making sure there are no lumps.

5. Assemble the lumpia: Scoop 5 tablespoons (52 grams) of the filling onto the center of a lumpia wrapper and shape into a horizontal line, all the way across the wrapper. Fold the bottom of the wrapper over the filling and start to roll tightly. Brush the flour paste on the top edge of the wrapper, then continue rolling to seal. Transfer to a baking sheet and repeat with the remaining wrappers and filling.

6. Cut each lumpia crosswise into 4 equal pieces.

7. If desired, arrange the lumpia in a single layer on a baking sheet, making sure they are not touching each other. Freeze until solid, 2–3 hours, then transfer to an airtight container. The lumpia will keep in the freezer for 3–4 weeks.

8. When ready to fry, pour 1 inch of canola oil into a large pot and heat over medium heat until the temperature reaches 375°F (190°C). Line a rimmed baking sheet with paper towels and set a wire rack on top.

9. Working in batches to avoid overcrowding the pot, add the lumpia to the hot oil and fry for 5–7 minutes, until golden brown. Transfer to the wire rack to drain and repeat with the remaining lumpia, allowing the oil to return to temperature between batches.

10. Serve the lumpia with your favorite sauce for dipping.

11. Enjoy!

Tasty's Purple Goddess

Ingredients

for 4 servings

SALAD

- 3 scallions, thinly sliced

- ¾ cup persian cucumber(110 g), finely chopped

- 2 tablespoons fresh dill, finely chopped, plus more for garnish

- ½ small head purple cabbage, finely chopped

- ½ red onion, finely chopped

- ¼ cup chives(10 g), thinly sliced, plus more for garnish

- 1 ½ teaspoons kosher salt

- blue corn tortilla chip, for serving

DRESSING

- 6 oz red beet(175 g), peeled and roasted

- 2 cloves garlic

- 1 small shallot, quartered

- ½ cup blackberry(75 g), fresh or frozen

- ½ cup fresh basil leaf(20 g), preferable opal basil

- ½ cup purple kale leaves(20 g), packed

- ¼ cup nutritional yeast(30 g)

- ⅓ cup lemon(80 mL), juiced

- 2 tablespoons olive oil

- 2 tablespoons cashews, or pine nuts

- 1 tablespoon balsamic vinegar

- 1 teaspoon kosher salt

- ½ teaspoon freshly ground black pepper

- water, as needed

Preparation

1. Make the salad: Add the scallions, cucumbers, dill, cabbage, red onion, chives, and salt to a large bowl and toss to combine. Let sit for 5–10 minutes while you make the dressing.

2. In a blender, combine the beets, garlic, shallot, blackberries, basil, kale, nutritional yeast, lemon juice, olive oil, cashews, 1 tablespoon balsamic vinegar, and 1 teaspoon salt. Blend until completely smooth, then add more

vinegar and salt to taste. Add 1–2 tablespoons of water as needed to loosen the dressing to your desired consistency.

3. Pour about half of the dressing over the salad and toss until evenly coated. Add more dressing as needed.

4. Transfer the salad to a serving bowl and top with more chives and dill, if desired. Serve immediately with the remaining dressing and blue corn chips alongside. The salad will keep in the refrigerator for up to 2 days.

5. Enjoy!

Jasmine's Snack Board

Ingredients

for 4 servings

PRAWN CRACKERS

- 2 cups canola oil(480 mL), for frying

- 1 box prawn-flavored chips

SPAM MUSUBI

- 2 tablespoons canola oil

- ½ can Spam®, halved lengthwise

- 2 tablespoons water

- 2 tablespoons soy sauce

- 2 tablespoons sugar, plus 2 teaspoons, divided

- ½ teaspoon kosher salt

- 2 tablespoons rice vinegar

- 1 ⅓ cups sushi rice(265 g), cooked

- 4 strips nori, 2 in (5 cm)

CALIFORNIA ROLL

- canola oil, for greasing

- 2 cups sushi rice(400 g), cooked, seasoned with 2 tablespoons of rice vinegar

- 8 pieces imitation crab

- 1 avocado, thinly sliced

- 1 small cucumber, cut into machsticks

- 4 sheets sushi-grade nori, 8½ x 7½

ASSEMBLY

- 1 package pan-fried dumplings, 24 ounce (700 G)

- 2 cups garlic edamame(320 g)

- 4 scallion pancakes, cut into triangles

- 1 large red dragon fruit, peeled and diced

- 4 pineapple cakes

- 4 probiotic yogurt drinks

- 8 pieces assorted mochi

- 1 loaf mujigae-tteok loaf, sliced

- 2 strawberry flavored Hello Panda cookies, 9 ounce (260 grams)

- 4 choco pies

- 1 cara cara orange, large, sliced

- 2 Mandarin orange slices

- 1 large asian pear, sliced

Preparation

1. Make the prawn crackers: Heat the oil in a large heavy-bottomed pan over medium heat until the temperature reaches 325°F (160°C). Line a plate with paper towels and set nearby.

2. Place 8–10 chips in a slotted spoon or spider. Gently lower them into the hot oil and stir gently. As the chips begin to float to the surface, quickly remove from the oil before they scorch or burn. Carefully shake off any excess oil, and then place on the lined plate. Continue frying the remaining chips.

3. Make the spam musubi: Heat the canola oil in a large nonstick skillet over medium-high heat. Add the Spam and cook for 2–3 minutes per side, until golden brown and crispy.

4. In a small bowl, whisk together the water, soy sauce, and 2 tablespoons of sugar.

5. Reduce the heat to low and pour the soy sauce mixture into the skillet. Cook until the sauce is bubbly and thick and coats the Spam evenly, turning as needed, about 5 minutes total. Remove the pan from the heat.

6. In a medium bowl, whisk together the remaining 2 teaspoons sugar, salt, and vinegar. Add the cooked sushi rice and stir to combine.

7. Lay a strip of nori, shiny side down, on a clean surface. Place the box of the musubi press on top. Add ⅓ cup of the seasoned rice to the box and press down with the plunger. Lay a piece of Spam on top of the rice and press down firmly. Lift the box to release the Spam and rice. Wrap the nori around the stack, using a wet finger to seal the nori.

8. Make the California rolls: Lightly grease the inner chamber of a sushi bazooka with canola oil.

9. Add ½ cup of the seasoned sushi rice to each half of the inner chamber and use the plunger to create a divot down the length of each side of rice. Arrange half of the crab, avocado, and cucumber in a horizontal row on one side of the rice. Carefully close the bazooka.

10. Lay a piece of nori, shiny side down, on the sushi mat. Turn the plunger 5 times, then firmly press to release the roll onto one end of the nori. Tightly roll the nori around the rice to completely encase the roll. Transfer the roll to a cutting board. Rub a knife on a damp paper towel before slicing the roll crosswise into 6 equal pieces. Repeat with the remaining ingredients to make another roll.

11. Assemble the board: Place the prawn crackers, musubi, and California rolls in the center of a turntable. Arrange the pan-fried dumplings, garlic edamame, scallion pancakes, dragonfruit, pineapple cakes, probiotic yogurt drinks, mochi, mujigae-tteok, Hello Panda cookies, Choco pies, Cara Cara and Mandarin oranges, and Asian pears around the edges.

12. Enjoy!

Pesto Chicken Low-carb Broccoli Parmesan Cups

Ingredients

for 12 servings

- 2 cups broccoli floret(300 g)

- 1 clove garlic, minced

- 1 cup grated parmesan cheese(110 g)

- 1 egg

- 2 tablespoons olive oil, divided

- 2 boneless, skinless chicken breasts, cubed

- salt, to taste

- pepper, to taste

- 1 cup pesto(230 g)

- 1 ½ cups cherry tomato(300 g), halved

- 1 tablespoon fresh basil, chopped

Preparation

1. Preheat oven to 375°F (190°C).

2. In a food processor add the broccoli, Parmesan, 1 clove of garlic, 1egg and 1 tablespoon of olive oil. Pulse until mixture forms a dough like texture, about 2 minutes.

3. Place 1 tablespoon of the broccoli mixture and press into a well greased muffin tin. Form the mixture into a cup, making the bottom and sides ½-inches (1 cm) thick.

4. Bake for about 30 minutes until the edges are golden and crispy and the bottom is firm.

5. Cool the broccoli cups. Once cooled, remove from the muffin tin.

6. Heat 1 tablespoon olive oil in a large skillet medium heat. Add the chicken and season with salt and pepper, and cook until golden on all sides.

7. Add the pesto and stir to combine. Remove from the heat.

8. Fill the broccoli Parmesan cups with the pesto chicken. Top with slices of tomatoes and basil.

9. Broccoli Parmesan Cups can be stored up to 3 days and can be reheated in the oven.

10. Enjoy!

Protein-Packed Breakfast Bars

Ingredients

for 24 bars

BASE

- ¼ cup flax meal(40 g)

- ¾ cup water(180 mL)

- 6 cups rolled oats(540 g)

- 6 cups quinoa(1 kg), cooked

- 4 teaspoons baking powder

- 1 teaspoon salt

- 1 cup maple syrup(220 g)

- ½ cup refined coconut oil(120 mL), melted

- 2 teaspoons vanilla extract

- 4 ripe bananas, mashed

FILLINGS

PEANUT BUTTER CHOCOLATE CHIP

- 6 tablespoons peanut butter

- 5 tablespoons mini chocolate chips

APPLE CINNAMON

- ¾ cup gala apple(90 g), diced

- 6 tablespoons walnuts, chopped

- 1 ½ tablespoons cinnamon

- ¼ teaspoon nutmeg

CARROT CAKE

- ¾ cup carrot(30 g), grated
- 3 teaspoons cinnamon
- ¼ teaspoon nutmeg
- 3 tablespoons almond butter

MIXED BERRY

- 3 tablespoons almond butter
- ⅓ cup Strawberries(55 g), diced
- ⅓ cup raspberries(40 g)
- ⅓ cup blueberries(40 g)
- nonstick cooking spray

Preparation

1. Preheat the oven to 375°F (190°C).

2. To make the flax eggs, combine the flax meal and water in a small bowl and mix well. Set aside for 10 minutes to gel.

3. In a large bowl, combine the oats, quinoa, baking powder, salt, maple syrup, coconut oil, vanilla, flax eggs, and bananas, and mix until well-combined.

4. Divide the base dough equally between 4 medium bowls.

5. Add the peanut butter and chocolate chips to 1 bowl and mix until combined.

6. Add the apple, walnuts, cinnamon, and nutmeg to another bowl and mix until combined.

7. Add the carrots, cinnamon, nutmeg, and almond butter to another bowl and mix until combined.

8. Add the almond butter, strawberries, raspberries, and blueberries to the last bowl and mix until combined.

9. Grease 2 9x13-inch (23x33-cm) baking pans with nonstick spray. Transfer the bar mixtures to the pans, packing each mixture into half of a pan with a spoon or spatula.

10. Bake for 25-30 minutes, until the edges are slightly golden brown.

11. Remove the pans from the oven and let the bars cool for 20 minutes, then refrigerate for at least 30 minutes, or up to 5 days. Gently cut each flavor into 6 bars, then remove from the pans with a spatula.

12. Enjoy!

Easy To Serve Chicken Parmesan Poppers

Ingredients

for 14 poppers

- 14 cherry peppers, whole pickled

- 14 balls mozzarella cheese

CHICKEN MIXTURE

- 1 lb ground chicken(455 g)

- 1 large egg, beaten

- 1 cup shredded parmesan cheese(100 g)

- ¼ cup milk(60 mL)

- ½ cup bread crumbs(55 g)

- ¼ medium yellow onion, minced

- 2 teaspoons fresh parsley, minced

- 1 teaspoon garlic powder

- 1 teaspoon pepper

- 1 teaspoon kosher salt

ASSEMBLY

- 1 cup bread crumbs(115 g)

- ¼ cup shredded parmesan cheese(25 g)

- 1 teaspoon dried parsley

- 1 teaspoon garlic powder

- 1 teaspoon kosher salt

- 3 large eggs

- 1 cup all-purpose flour(125 g)

- canola oil, for frying

- 2 cups marinara sauce(520 g)

- 4 slices mozzarella cheese, cut into quarters

- fresh parsley, chopped, for garnish

Preparation

1. Drain and dry the pickled cherry peppers, then cut off the tops and use a teaspoon to scoop out the seeds. Place a mozzarella ball inside of each one.

2. Make the chicken mixture: In a large bowl, combine the ground chicken, egg, Parmesan, milk, bread crumbs, onion, parsley, garlic powder, pepper, and salt. Mix well.

3. Take a golf ball-size amount of the chicken mixture and pat it out flat in your palm. Place a stuffed cherry pepper in the center and wrap the chicken mixture around it until completely covered, rolling into a ball. Repeat with the remaining cherry peppers.

4. Chill for 20 minutes.

5. Preheat the oven to 450°F (230°C).

6. Prepare for frying: Add the bread crumbs to a medium bowl with the Parmesan, dried parsley, garlic powder, and salt. Beat the eggs in a separate medium bowl. Add the flour to another medium bowl.

7. Toss a chicken meatball in the flour, then coat in the eggs, then roll in the bread crumbs. Repeat with remaining meatballs.

8. Heat a large pan with ¼ inch (6 ml) of canola oil over medium-high heat until the oil reaches 400°F (200°C).

9. Working in batches, fry the chicken meatballs for 1-2 minutes on each side, or until light golden brown. Once finished, blot dry with paper towels and transfer to a greased baking sheet.

10. Dollop 1 tablespoon of marinara sauce on each ball, then top with a piece of mozzarella cheese.

11. Bake for 8 minutes, or until meatballs are cooked through with an internal temperature of 165°F (75°C).

12. Sprinkle with parsley and serve.

13. Enjoy!

Pizza Nachos

Ingredients

for 6 servings

- all-purpose flour, for dusting

- 14 oz pizza dough(395 g)

- ¼ cup olive oil(60 mL)

- 1 tablespoon McCormick® Oregano Leaves

- 2 teaspoons McCormick® Garlic Powder

- ½ teaspoon McCormick® Crushed Red Pepper

- 1 cup marinara sauce(260 g)

- 1 cup shredded mozzarella cheese(200 g)

- 10 pepperoni slice

- 1 lb mild italian sausage(455 g), cooked

- 1 cup cherry tomato(200 g), halved

- ½ cup parmesan cheese(55 g), freshly grated

- ¼ cup fresh basil leaf(10 g), torn

Preparation

1. Preheat the oven to 400°F (200°C). Line a baking sheet with parchment paper.

2. Lightly flour a clean surface. Roll out the pizza dough and cut into 4 strips, then cut each strip into 8 triangles. Transfer the triangles to the prepared baking sheet.

3. In a small bowl, whisk together the olive oil, oregano, garlic powder and crushed red pepper.

4. Brush the seasoned oil over the pizza dough triangles.

5. Bake for 10 minutes, or until the chips are crispy and golden brown. Remove the chips from the oven and leave the oven on.

6. Layer half of the chips in a large cast iron skillet or on a baking sheet. Spoon on half of the marinara sauce, then top with half of the mozzarella, pepperoni, Italian sausage, and tomatoes. Layer on the remaining ingredients.

7. Bake for 5 minutes, or until the cheese is melted.

8. Top the nachos with freshly grated Parmesan cheese and the basil, then serve.

9. Enjoy!

Chicken Salad Crostini

Ingredients

for 12 crostini

- 12 slices baguette, 1/2 in (1 cm), cut on a slight diagonal
- extra virgin olive oil, to taste
- kosher salt, to taste
- 24 slices green apple, thin
- 1 cup Waldorf chicken salad(100 g)
- 2 tablespoons walnuts, chopped and toasted

WALDORF CHICKEN SALAD

- 1 cup shredded chicken breast(125 g)
- 2 tablespoons red grapes, halved
- 2 tablespoons celery, finely chopped
- 2 tablespoons mayonnaise

- 2 teaspoons lemon juice

- salt, to taste

- pepper, to taste

Preparation

1. Preheat the oven to 425°F (220°C). Line a baking sheet with parchment paper.

2. Arrange the bread in a single layer on the prepared baking sheet. Brush each piece of bread with olive oil. Lightly sprinkle with salt. Bake for 12-14 minutes, until the edges are light golden brown. Let cool.

3. Make the Waldorf chicken salad: In a medium bowl, combine the chicken breast, grapes, celery, mayonnaise, and lemon juice and mix well. Season with salt and pepper.

4. Place 2 apple slices on each crostini. Top with 1 heaping tablespoon of chicken salad. Garnish with ½ teaspoon chopped walnuts.

5. Enjoy!

Easy Shrimp Ceviche

Ingredients

for 2 cups

- 10 limes

- 1 lb shrimp(455 g), peeled, deveined, and diced

- 2 teaspoons kosher salt

- 2 jalapeñoes, seeded and minced

- 1 small red onion, diced

- 2 cups cherry tomato(400 g), chopped

- fresh cilantro leaf, for garnish, optional

- tortilla chip, for serving

Preparation

1. Halve the limes, then juice using a citrus press or a pair of kitchen tongs. You should have about 1 cup (240 ML) total.

2. In a medium bowl, combine the shrimp, lime juice, salt, jalapeños, onion, and tomatoes. Mix well.

3. Cover and refrigerate for about 4 hours, until the shrimp is opaque and firm.

4. Serve the ceviche chilled. Garnish with cilantro, if desired, and serve with tortilla chips.

5. Enjoy!

Bacon Cheddar Deviled Eggs

Ingredients

for 6 servings

- 6 eggs

- 3 tablespoons mayonnaise

- 1 teaspoon apple cider vinegar

- ¼ teaspoon kosher salt

- 1 teaspoon French's yellow mustard

- 2 scallions, thinly sliced

- 2 strips bacon, cooked and coarsely chopped

- ¼ cup shredded cheddar cheese (25 g)

- freshly ground black pepper

Preparation

1. Place eggs in a small saucepan. Add cold water to the pot to completely submerge the eggs. Bring to a boil, then cover pot with a lid and turn off the heat. Let eggs sit in the hot water for 14 minutes.

2. Transfer the eggs to a bowl of ice water to cool. Peel the eggs.

3. Slice eggs in half lengthwise and carefully remove the yolks. Transfer the yolks to a mixing bowl and set aside the halved egg whites.

4. Mash the yolks with a fork until crumbly. Stir in the mayonnaise, vinegar, salt, and French's Yellow Mustard until the filling is smooth.

5. Transfer the filling to a piping bag and pipe into the halved egg whites.

6. Top the deviled eggs with the scallions, bacon, and cheddar cheese, dividing evenly. Top with freshly ground pepper and serve.

7. Enjoy!

Pizza Sticks 3 Ways

Ingredients

for 24 pizza sticks

PEPPERONI PIZZA STICKS

- ¼ cup extra virgin olive oil(60 mL)

- ½ teaspoon garlic powder

- ½ teaspoon italian seasoning

- all purpose flour, for dusting

- 1 tube refrigerated pizza dough, 13.8 ounce (390 G)

- 40 slices pepperoni slices

- 2 tablespoons grated parmesan cheese

- pizza sauce, for serving

VEGETARIAN PIZZA STICKS

- 8 oz cremini mushroom(225 g), cleaned and quartered

- ½ medium red onion, diced

- 1 green bell pepper, seeded and diced

- kosher salt, to taste

- black pepper, to taste

- ¼ teaspoon red pepper flakes

- ¼ cup extra virgin olive oil(60 mL), divided

- 1 tube refrigerated pizza dough, 13.8 ounce (390 G)

- ½ cup shredded mozzarella cheese(50 g)

- ranch dressing, for serving

MARGHERITA PIZZA STICKS

- 40 cherry tomatoes

- 1 tube refrigerated pizza dough, 13.8 ounce (390 G)

- 2 tablespoons extra virgin olive oil

- ½ cup shredded mozzarella cheese(50 g)

- chopped fresh basil, chopped, for garnish

- pesto, for serving

SPECIAL EQUIPMENT

- 24 wooden skewers, 12 in (30 cm)

Preparation

1. Soak the wooden skewers in water for at least 30 minutes to prevent burning.

2. Preheat the oven to 400°F (200°C) and line 4 baking sheets, or as many as you have, with parchment paper.

3. Make the pepperoni pizza sticks: In a small bowl, whisk together the olive oil, garlic powder, and Italian seasoning. Set aside.

4. Unroll the pizza dough on a lightly floured surface and cut into 8 strips.

5. Fold 5 pepperoni slices into quarters and thread onto a wooden skewer, spacing about 1 inch (2 ½ cm) apart. Repeat to make 8 skewers total.

6. Starting at the pointed end of a skewer, weave a dough strip down around the pepperoni slices, pinching at the bottom to secure, and set on a prepared baking sheet. Repeat with the remaining skewers.

7. Brush the skewers with the seasoned oil and sprinkle with the Parmesan cheese.

8. Bake the skewers for 10-12 minutes, rotating halfway through, until the dough is golden brown.

9. Serve with pizza sauce for dipping.

10. Make the vegetarian pizza sticks: Spread the mushrooms, onion, and bell pepper in an even layer on a baking sheet. Season with salt, pepper, and the red pepper flakes and drizzle with 2 tablespoons of olive oil. Toss to coat.

11. Roast the vegetables for 15 minutes, until the mushrooms are golden brown. Remove from the oven and set aside to cool.

12. Unroll the pizza dough on a lightly floured surface and cut into 8 strips.

13. Thread 1 piece of each vegetable onto the skewers to make 1 stack, spacing the stacks about 1 inch (2 ½ cm) apart (you should have about 4 stacks per skewer). Repeat to make 8 skewers total.

14. Starting at the pointed end of the skewer, weave a dough strip down around the vegetables, pinching at the bottom to secure, and set on a prepared baking sheet. Repeat with the remaining skewers.

15. Brush the skewers with the remaining 2 tablespoons of oil and sprinkle with the mozzarella cheese.

16. Bake the skewers for 10-12 minutes, rotating halfway through, until the dough is golden brown.

17. Serve with ranch dressing for dipping.

18. Make the margherita pizza skewers: Unroll the pizza dough on a lightly floured surface and cut into 8 strips.

19. Thread 5 cherry tomatoes onto a skewer, spacing about 1 inch (2 ½ cm) apart. Repeat to make 8 skewers total.

20. Starting at the pointed end of the skewer, weave a dough strip down around the tomatoes, pinching at the bottom to secure, and set on a prepared baking sheet. Repeat with the remaining skewers.

21. Brush the skewers with the olive oil and sprinkle with the mozzarella cheese.

22. Bake the skewers for 10-12 minutes, rotating halfway through, until the dough is golden brown.

23. Garnish with the basil and serve with pesto for dipping.

24. Enjoy!

Rainbow Kettle Corn

Ingredients

for 10 cups

- 12 tablespoons sugar, divided

- red gel food coloring

- orange gel food coloring

- yellow gel food coloring

- green gel food coloring

- blue food coloring

- purple gel food coloring

- 6 teaspoons coconut oil, divided

- 12 tablespoons white popcorn kernels, divided, plus 12 kernels

- 1 ½ teaspoons kosher salt, divided

Preparation

1. Line a baking sheet with parchment paper.

2. Divide the sugar evenly between 6 small bowls, 2 tablespoons per bowl.

3. Dye each bowl of sugar a different color by adding 1-2 drops of red, orange, yellow, green, blue and purple food coloring. Stir each bowl with a clean fork until the sugars are sandy in texture. Note: We recommend gel food coloring, as the colors are more stable. Only use 1-2 drops; a little goes a long way.

4. Add 1 teaspoon of coconut oil and 2 popcorn kernels to a medium nonstick saucepan with a lid. Cover and place over medium-high heat. Once the kernels pop, reduce the heat to medium and add 2 tablespoons of popcorn kernels and 1 bowl of colored sugar. Immediately cover the pan and shake to combine. Cook, shaking the pan constantly to ensure that the sugar doesn't burn, while the popcorn pops. Once the pops are more than 3 seconds apart, remove the pot from heat. Carefully remove the lid away from your body and pour the popcorn onto the prepared baking sheet.

5. Evenly sprinkle ¼ teaspoon salt over the hot kettle corn. Let the popcorn cool completely, transfer to a bowl. Repeat with the remaining colors, replacing the parchment paper as needed.

6. Combine all of the popcorn in a large bowl. Toss to distribute the colors evenly. Serve immediately, or store in an airtight container for up to 2 days.

7. Enjoy!

6. Factors That May Impact Bipolar Health

Genetics, brain chemistry, the environment, and one's way of life are only few of the elements that have been linked to the development of bipolar illness. The health of someone with bipolar disorder may be affected by the following:

There is a substantial hereditary component to bipolar illness, making those with a family history of the disorder more vulnerable to experiencing symptoms themselves. However, it is not fully understood which genes have a role in bipolar illness, and it is possible that other variables, such as environmental ones, play a part as well.

Dopamine, serotonin, and norepinephrine are just few of the neurotransmitters that have been linked to chemical abnormalities in people with bipolar illness. Mood, vitality, and other mental health factors can all be impacted by chemical imbalances.

Symptoms of bipolar disorder can be triggered or made worse by exposure to environmental variables such as stress, trauma, and substance addiction. Mood can be unstable when sleep is disrupted or when circadian rhythms are altered.

Finding the best medicine or drug regimen for controlling bipolar illness is often crucial. It might take time and effort to discover the proper drug and dose, but doing so can help stabilize mood, lessen symptoms, and avoid recurrence.

Diet, physical activity, and enough rest can all have an effect on the mental health of those with bipolar disorder. Maintaining regular exercise and sleep habits together with a healthy, balanced diet may do wonders for your health and your mental state.

Individuals with bipolar illness are more likely to experience the emergence of co-occurring problems, including anxiety and drug use disorders. These comorbidities can make it more challenging to treat bipolar disorder and control associated symptoms.

As we have shown, factors like as genetics, brain chemistry, environment, medication management, lifestyle, and co-occurring disorders can all play a role in a person's risk of developing bipolar disorder. It is essential to collaborate with a healthcare provider to create a holistic treatment plan that takes into account all of these elements and includes regular check-ins and follow-ups. Many persons with bipolar illness are able to attain and maintain stability and enhance their quality of life with the help of medication and management.

Sleep

Bipolar persons, like everyone else, benefit greatly from adequate sleep hygiene practices. Some people with bipolar illness have sleeplessness, while others experience the opposite problem—hypersomnia. Sleep disturbances exacerbate bipolar symptoms and can set off manic episodes. Among the many ways in which sleep affects bipolar health are:

- Mood modulation through sleep: People with bipolar illness are particularly vulnerable to the effects that sleep disruption can have on their mood. Manic or hypomanic episodes can be triggered by a lack of sleep, whereas depressed episodes can be triggered by too much sleep. Getting a good night's sleep is crucial for maintaining a stable mood and avoiding mood swings.

- Bipolar illness patients need more sleep to get the most out of their medication. Mood stabilizers and antipsychotics, two common classes of drugs used to treat bipolar illness, can have sedative effects. Taking these meds before bed can increase their efficacy and provide for a better night's sleep.

- The quality of your sleep can be enhanced and the likelihood of mood episodes reduced by practicing excellent sleep hygiene. Some examples of good sleep hygiene are sticking to a regular sleep schedule, avoiding stimulating activities in the hours before bed, and making your bedroom a relaxing place to unwind.

- Significance of Sleep Disturbance: Mood episodes can be predicted by shifts in sleep habits. Paying attention to shifts in sleep habits can alert people with bipolar disease to impending mood episodes, allowing them to take preventative measures.

- The therapeutic value of sleep: Treatment for bipolar illness must include adequate rest. Insomnia sufferers who undergo cognitive-behavioral therapy for insomnia (CBT-I) have shown improvement in sleep quality and symptom severity, making this kind of psychotherapy a promising option for the treatment of bipolar disorder. Bipolar disorder medicines, such as sedatives and sleep aids, can sometimes improve sleep quality.

Sleep plays an important role in the management of bipolar disease, and sleep disruptions can exacerbate symptoms and precipitate mood episodes. The health and well-being of people with bipolar illness can be improved via the practice of good sleep hygiene, the recognition of changes in sleep patterns as warning indicators, and the incorporation of sleep into treatment programs.

Stress

Bipolar illness patients are more vulnerable to the negative effects of stress on their health. Mania, hypomania, and depression are the two main symptoms of bipolar disorder, which is a mental health disease. The frequency and severity of these mood swings might be exacerbated by stress. Some of the ways that stress might worsen bipolar health are listed below.

- Stress can set off manic or depressive episodes in people with bipolar illness. An increase in the frequency or severity of manic or depressed episodes is one possible consequence.

- Stress can exacerbate the difficulties experienced by people with bipolar illness in controlling their symptoms. Sleeplessness, worry, and other mental and emotional symptoms may result.

- The efficacy of medicines for bipolar illness may also be affected by stress. A decrease in the efficacy of mood stabilizers due to stress may increase the frequency of mood episodes.

- Stress may raise the risk of drug abuse for those with bipolar illness. Using substances like alcohol or drugs as a crutch during times of stress can exacerbate symptoms and increase the likelihood of mood disorders.

- Stress can have negative effects on daily functioning, including academic and social performance. As a result, the severity of symptoms and the likelihood of mood episodes might be further exacerbated.

Stress management is a crucial component of treatment for bipolar illness. Exercise, deep breathing, meditation, eating well, and getting enough sleep are just some of the stress-management strategies available. When you need help, it's crucial to reach out to friends and family or a mental health expert. In addition, those who suffer from bipolar illness may do well to devise a strategy for dealing with stressful situations, particularly at times of high stress or big life transitions, when they are more likely to experience a mood episode.

Exercise

People with bipolar illness might benefit from regular exercise. Regular exercise can aid in the management of symptoms for both sadness and mania, which are both connected with bipolar illness.

Exercising has been demonstrated to help persons with bipolar disease by elevating their mood, decreasing stress, and boosting happiness. The quality of sleep, which is commonly disturbed in persons with bipolar illness, can also be improved via exercise.

Exercising has been shown to improve mental health and, in some cases, physical health as well. Cardiovascular disease is a major risk factor in bipolar illness, although regular exercise can help lower that risk.

Anxiety and stress are common co-occurring disorders with bipolar illness, and regular exercise can help alleviate their symptoms. Regular exercise has been shown to be as helpful as medicine for the treatment of anxiety and depression, according to a number of studies.

However, it's crucial to remember that physical activity isn't meant to replace medication or other therapies for bipolar disease. Treatment plans, which may include medication, counseling, and lifestyle modifications like exercise, should be developed in collaboration with a healthcare professional.

It's also wise to ease into your workout regimen and work your way up to your desired level of intensity. Some persons with bipolar illness experience a manic episode when they overdo it. A doctor or other medical professional can help you figure out the best and safest way to get in shape.

Persons with bipolar illness can benefit from engaging in regular physical activity. Positive effects on mood, stress levels, and physical well-being are all possible. However, it is best taken in conjunction with other therapies and under the supervision of a medical professional.

Suggestions for incorporating lifestyle changes to support bipolar health

Making certain adjustments to your daily routine can have a significant impact on your mental health and quality of life if you suffer from bipolar illness. Here are a few recommendations:

- Be consistent: Developing a regular schedule might help you feel more at ease and get better rest. Aim for a daily routine that includes a set time to get up, eat, and go to bed.

- Regular physical activity: Depression and anxiety are often alleviated, along with general mood, by engaging in regular physical activity. Exercise for at least 30 minutes every day, most days of the week.

- Maintain a wholesome diet: Boost your disposition and stamina with the aid of a diet full of fruits, vegetables, nutritious grains, and lean protein. Cut back on the junk food and sugary treats.

- Get plenty of shut-eye. Bipolar illness patients who don't get enough sleep are more likely to experience mood swings. Get between seven and nine hours of sleep every night, and make sure you have a regular routine in place to help you unwind before bed.

- Relaxation practices like meditation, deep breathing, or yoga can help people with bipolar disease deal with stress, which can cause mood episodes.

- Don't drink or use drugs; they might make it harder to take your meds or perhaps induce a mood crisis. If you have a problem with substance misuse, you should avoid these substances and look for treatment.

- Avoid isolating yourself; social isolation and loneliness can amplify the negative effects of bipolar disease. It might also be beneficial to participate in social activities or join a support group.

To manage bipolar illness, medication and treatment are essential; lifestyle modifications should not be used instead. However, if you're willing to make some adjustments, you may find that your therapy and general quality of life improve as a result. If you want specific advice on how to improve your bipolar health through lifestyle modifications, talk to your doctor.

Made in the USA
Coppell, TX
26 August 2024

36506984R00184